PRAISE FOR *Everything*

"No one closes this book unchanged. It ennobles desires. It releases dreams."

—Leonard Sweet, best-selling author, professor at Drew University and George Fox University, and Chief Contributor to Sermons.com

"More than ever, we crave spiritual leadership not from academics in ivory towers but from battle-tested disciples in the trenches. This is the trusted counselor we find in Mary DeMuth. With wisdom and experience and tenderness and beauty, she leads us closer to Jesus in *Everything*—through despair, past fear, beyond control, and all the way to surrender."

—Jen Hatmaker, best-selling author of *Interrupted* and *7: An Experimental Mutiny Against Excess*

"In *Everything*, Mary DeMuth gives an honest and touching account of the journey she has taken to bring her out of despair and into God's glory. She embraces her vulnerabilities and flaws as stepping stones that have shaped her into a mighty woman of God. This book is an amazing testimony of the power of Jesus Christ to transform lives. I highly recommend this book to believers new and old who are in need of a fresh perspective on their circumstances."

—Pastor Matthew Barnett, cofounder of the Dream Center

"Let's be honest. Most of us who follow Christ are holding back. We want Christ but are convinced we'll miss something if we surrender everything. In this challenging but tender book, Mary DeMuth invites us to give Him *everything* in order to experience Him as *Everything*. In the end, it is the only course that will satisfy our deepest longings."

—Michael Hyatt, *New York Times* best-selling author of *Platform* and former CEO, Thomas Nelson Publishers

"Mary DeMuth asks us to live fully vulnerable, honest and raw with head, heart, and hands as we give our lives to a God who takes our failures and creates successes, our mistakes and makes them into growth and our worries into capabilities. Mary welcomes us to live this 'everything life' by telling her stories in beautiful snapshots of a real and accessible life."

—Sarah Markley, blogger, freelance writer, and speaker

"In *Everything*, Mary takes us back to the heart of our faith. She reminds us what it means to surrender everything in order to gain everything; in order to gain true freedom. . . . it's a r................d not forget."

.h Mae, coauthor of *Desperate*

"Mary DeMuth beautifully weaves theology with poetry, which makes this book hard to put down. I was struck by the brilliance of her thoughts and overwhelmed by the power of her words. *Everything* is an honest, passionate account of one soul's thirst for God, and reading it will stir up your hunger—and then satisfy you."

—Jeff Goins, author of *Wrecked: When a Broken World Slams into Your Comfortable Life*

"With [Mary DeMuth's] great storytelling, personal vulnerability, and scriptural insights she leads us to the paradox of life and eternity: Jesus asks us to give EVERYTHING to Him. And then He turns around and gives us EVERYTHING—and more—than we could ever need or desire. What a trade! I'll take it."

—Judy Douglass, author, speaker, encourager, Office of the President, Campus Crusade for Christ International (Cru)

"I judge a book's impact based on how much I underline as I read. *Everything* has something underlined on nearly every page. It is a book filled with wisdom, yet written from a vulnerable heart."

—Marybeth Whalen, author of *The Guest Book*, *She Makes It Look Easy* and *The Mailbox*; founder of SheReads.org

"Mary is a fresh and needed voice. . . . Mary brings a fresh perspective to living out faith in the details of everyday life that is both challenging and inspiring. I highly recommend *Everything*. Your walk with Christ—and your life—may never be the same."

—Carey Nieuwhof, author of *Leading Change Without Losing It* and *Parenting Beyond Your Capacity*, lead pastor of Connexus Church

"In *Everything*, DeMuth weaves words, verses, and stories to show us how to grow and truly live, how to give and gain a wholehearted life in Christ."

—Rachel Olsen, author of *It's No Secret* and coauthor of *My One Word: Change Your Life with Just One Word*

"*Everything* is refreshing, exciting, convicting, and encouraging. . . . *Everything* is life-changing at the very core of our being."

—Mick Ukleja, PhD, consultant, speaker, coach, author, and chairman of the board of trustees, the Astronauts Memorial Foundation, Kennedy Space Center

"*Everything* is everything you could ask for in a personal primer on how to walk closely with Christ. . . . No cookie cutter spiritual answers here—just pure inspiration for forging a close walk with Jesus in the midst of the mess of life."

—Karen Ehman, Proverbs 31 Ministries Director of Speakers, author of *Let. It. Go*

"I have no doubt that God will use Mary DeMuth to reach millions as she speaks the truth we so desperately need to keep our spirits sensitive to everything God is and our hearts thankful for everything God provides."

—Allison Bottke, founder of SANITY Support and best-selling author of the *Setting Boundaries* book series

"Everyone who knows Mary agrees on these two things: She's real in her writing and relentless in the way she runs after her Savior. . . . With raw honesty, Mary opens up her story. And with gritty grace she helps you embrace your own story, to believe it can be redeemed. Read and be reminded that God is abundantly able to set you free to be *everything* He intended you to be."

—Susie Larson, radio host of *Live the Promise* and author of *The Uncommon Woman* and *Your Beautiful Purpose*

"Mary DeMuth has learned a valuable secret—that surrender is what truly leads to victory. . . . Mary's voice, heart, and passion for Jesus will guide you into greater freedom and joy on these pages."

—Holley Gerth, best-selling author of *You're Already Amazing*

"With an abundance of Scripture and excellent discussion questions, Mary DeMuth's book *Everything* makes for a perfect small group book study. Mary's storytelling style with a depth of life experiences kept me engaged throughout."

—Mark Randall, chaplain of Athletes in Action and minister at Evangelical Church Alliance

"Mary DeMuth writes like a friend, like a fellow struggler and straggler and I find myself nodding the whole way through—a perfect book to put in the 'truths I don't want to forget' section of your library."

—Emily P. Freeman, author of *Grace for the Good Girl*

"I always learn from a person who pulls the shades up on their life—shares the struggles, the growth, the lessons with courage. Mary DeMuth does this, in her book *Everything*. There is so much truth in the pages . . . so much Jesus. . . This is Mary's best non-fiction work yet."

—Lisa Whittle, Compassion advocate, speaker, and author of {w}hole and *Behind Those Eyes*

"As a fan of Mary DeMuth, I was hoping *Everything* would inspire and challenge me. It did that, but it went deeper. Mary's words touched wounds in my heart I hadn't realized were there and brought healing to ragged places. I read the whole book in less than a week, and I'm pretty sure 1/4 of every page is highlighted. This is a book that will remain on my bookshelf—one I'll refer to often. . . . Loved this book!"

—Tricia Goyer, author of 32 books, including *Blue Like Play Dough*

"Mary DeMuth knows both the cost and the joy of making Jesus her everything. With humility and transparency, she combines personal stories, practical suggestions, and solid biblical teaching to inspire readers to do the same. I highly recommend this book to anyone who longs for the adventure, the depth, and the fulfillment that wholehearted devotion to Christ brings."

—Grace Fox, international speaker, national codirector of International Messengers Canada, and author of *Moving from Fear to Freedom: A Woman's Guide to Peace in Every Situation*

"When Mary DeMuth writes, we pay attention. Why? Because Mary writes about struggles that lie close to the heart of Everyman. . . . It is her vulnerability that woos us to come alongside her on this journey toward an *everything* kind of life."

—Missy Buchanan, coauthor with Robin Roberts (*Good Morning America*),
My Story, My Song: Mother-Daughter Reflections on Life and Faith

"If you're ready to live wholeheartedly for God, releasing all you have and all you are, Mary DeMuth is the doula whose wise and beautiful words will draw you into life that really is life."

—Margot Starbuck, author of *Small Things With Great
Love: Adventures in Loving Your Neighbor*

"Mary DeMuth writes with a raw honesty that invites you to bring your own pain and secrets out of hiding and into the light so that you may be healed. . . . *Everything* needs to have a place in the library of every Christian I know. Read this book—it will change you for the better."

—Shannon Primicerio, author and speaker

"Everyone should read *Everything*. Well, anyone interested in deepening their relationship with and increasing their faith in Jesus Christ, at least. With razor-sharp storytelling and life-lived, Spirit-infused wisdom, DeMuth offers hope and encouragement and a path toward *everything* God intends for us."

—Caryn Rivadeneira, author of *Grumble Hallelujah*

"The message of *Everything* is both all-encompassing command and incomparable promise: If you want everything Jesus has to offer, release everything to Him. . . . The beauty of Mary DeMuth is she doesn't invite us to the *Everything* life without first living it herself."

—Michele Cushatt, speaker and author

"Mary gives each of us license to admit when things are hard and follows it up with encouragement to keep walking. This book met me in brokenness and walked with me into healing."

—Allison Johnston, speaker and life coach, allisonjohnston.org, @raisingthedead

I've been humbly blessed to have more
endorsements than page space. To read more, go to:
www.marydemuth.com/everythingthebook/endorsements/

everything

what you give and
what you gain
to become like Jesus

MARY
DEMUTH

THOMAS NELSON
Since 1798

NASHVILLE   DALLAS   MEXICO CITY   RIO DE JANEIRO

To Patrick, my lifeline, theological coach, and best friend

Published in Nashville, Tennessee, by Thomas Nelson. Thomas Nelson is a trademark of Thomas Nelson, Inc.

Thomas Nelson, Inc., titles may be purchased in bulk for educational, business, fund-raising, or sales promotional use. For information, please e-mail SpecialMarkets@ThomasNelson.com.

Published in association with the literary agency of Fedd & Company, Inc., Post Office Box 341973, Austin, TX 78734.

Page design by Walter Petrie

Library of Congress Cataloging-in-Publication Data

DeMuth, Mary E., 1967–
 Everything : what you give and what you gain to be more like Jesus / Mary DeMuth.
  p. cm.
 Includes bibliographical references.
 ISBN 978-1-4002-0398-7
 1. Spiritual formation. I. Title.
 BV4511.D45 2012
 248.4—dc23   2012008462

Printed in the United States of America

12 13 14 15 16 QG 6 5 4 3 2 1

∂ Contents

THE EVERYTHING JOURNEY

*Spiritual growth is more than a procedure; it's a wild
search for God in the tangled jungle of our souls.*

—MICHAEL YACONELLI[1]

TWO SNAPSHOTS—A CONTINENT AND AN ERA APART.

SNAPSHOT ONE

"I feel crushed," I told my husband, Patrick. I recalled the scene in the
vibrant colors of southern France in 2004. I could almost taste the *pain
au chocolat*. I smelled the warmth wafting through our upstairs loft of
a bedroom. Tucked (crammed) in the corner of the room sat my desk
where I wrote my first few books.

I propped myself against the pillows on our bed, arms crossed across
my chest. I felt the heaviness. Tasted it.

He held my hand. I sensed his worry about me because he entwined
my fingers lightly, tenderness and desperation mixed together in his
touch. "What do you mean?" broke the brief silence.

I chose to ignore his question, not out of anger, not because I wanted to dismiss him, but because so little was left of me that I couldn't even form a response. "Why is God doing this to me? How long will He ask us to endure?"

Patrick's theological words helped. God is sovereign. God is good. God sees. He is more than our emotions. Regardless of our desperation, He will work.

I nodded while tears tickled my cheeks. "I'm tired," I said. "So tired." I know he felt he had lost me, and in truth he had. Gone was the innovative Mary who wanted to conquer the world for Jesus. Gone was the girl who loved to talk to people, who relished new relationships around the dinner table, who attempted triathlons. She vanished into the salty sweet air of the Mediterranean, replaced by a frightened, broken, torn-up girl who no longer felt heroic.

Looking back, I see our two and a half years in France as compacting. Pressing. I am Princess Leia in the garbage chute, the walls closing in, moving ever closer to my skin, my bones, my heart. And just as I hope the metal will clank to a stop, they press further still, crushing everything about me.

That's how I felt as I sat on the bed, arms crossed, heart crushed. I spilled out all my words in that moment. Faithless words. "Why would God do this to us? Why would He call us here only to pulverize us? Why can't anything go right?"

Patrick listened to the words.

I remembered that psalm where David echoed me. Psalm 13:1–4:

> *How long, O LORD? Will you forget me forever?*
> *How long will you hide your face from me?*
> *How long must I take counsel in my soul*
> *and have sorrow in my heart all the day?*
> *How long shall my enemy be exalted over me?*
> *Consider and answer me, O LORD my God;*
> *light up my eyes, lest I sleep the sleep of death,*

lest my enemy say, "I have prevailed over him,"
lest my foes rejoice because I am shaken.

David's melodic words mimicked mine. So shockingly mine. In that moment on the bed, I could not dream of a better life. Ahead I saw only more strife and pain and darkness. I lived bereft of hope. I slipped into fury when I read the last two verses:

But I have trusted in your steadfast love;
my heart shall rejoice in your salvation.
I will sing to the LORD,
because he has dealt bountifully with me. (vv. 5–6)

Bountiful became a foreign word to me in France, though the countryside boasted otherwise. Grapes and lavender and sunflowers shouted their joy while I wilted and shook.

Have you ever felt that way? Where everything you build crumbles? Where your dreams and expectations obliterate? Where growth stagnates?

SNAPSHOT TWO

I raised my hands skyward, the words of the worship song filtering through me. I sang surrounded by my church family in Texas, five years post-France. God's question whispered with the cadence of the song. "Would you trade France?" He asked.

Tears wept down cheeks, yet I smiled.

Would I?

Flashes of our time there pelted me. The team trauma. Our children crying as they trudged to French classrooms where belittling teachers made fun of them. Spiritual warfare thicker than reality— overt attacks against our family and each child. Losing our house in Texas to a con man, forced to succumb to foreclosure thousands of miles away. Language stress that strangled my tongue at the over-crowded grocery store. Not being heard. Suffering for what was right, but no one seeing. Leaving France defeated. So many trials stacked upon each other.

I remembered telling a veteran Christian our story. His elderly eyes had observed everything in ministry. I expected him to listen to our story, wisely nod his head, and say, "Yeah, that's ministry." But he didn't. He shook his head and said, "I've never heard of a story like yours. You went through far more than what seems possible." His words validated the pain.

"Nothing significant in the kingdom of God happens unless death occurs."

I thought about another wise man loving us with his words. We were fresh off the mission field, shell-shocked, exhausted. He listened to the story, paused, thought, then said, "Nothing significant in the kingdom of God happens unless death occurs."

I tasted that death. It took years to reboot my passion in ministry's aftermath.

So when God asked me, "Would you trade France?" all these pictures coagulated into one painful mosaic of memory.

And yet.

And yet, I can't deny the growth in the aftermath. Growth that once hibernated in the land of *c'est la vie* exploded on American soil like a hyperactive fireworks show. All that growth birthed from a time I felt pressed beyond recognition, where my ability to control my life died. Beneath France's dirt, I am a tiny green sprout emanating from a seed, still entombed by earth.

That's where becoming like Jesus starts, and that's where it ends. The soil. The darkness where death reigns and life begins. Roots reach for water while something imperceptible pushes life toward the warmth.

If I were to ask you when you acted the most like Jesus, my hunch is that you wouldn't say, "When all was perfect, when life felt controlled and manageable." No, you and I would sit across from each other in a coffee shop and tell harrowing stories of danger, stress, worry, loss, and disappointment. I'd tell my ministry story, and you'd share your story full of conflict and villains and devastation. We'd both agree that we grew in those circumstances like Virginia creeper after a rainstorm, though we couldn't see it at the time.

Recently I asked this question on my Facebook page: "When has God seemed closest to you?" What surprised me was that folks overwhelmingly cited trials. Here's a sampling:

- During labor when my preemie daughter was born.
- During the illness and death of my mother and sister.
- When I found out I was adopted.
- Waiting to see if my dad survived a horrific motorcycle accident.
- When I had a heart attack at thirty-eight years old.
- During my separation.
- Since the suicide of my spouse.
- When I was hospitalized for mental illness at a psychiatric hospital at sixteen.

Ironic, isn't it? God's nearness and the growth that happens in His light come from the very things we desire to flee.

- We grow when the walls press in.
- We grow when life steals our control.
- We grow in the darkness.

Lights on, hands raised, chin upturned, I rolled around God's question about trading France. I saw how settled I'd become, not in a place per se, but in my heart. I perceived how secure I'd become, more apt to walk in good theology, genuinely believing God holds the entire universe under His sovereign control. I was less prone to despair. I prayed more, trusted more, believed more, relinquished more. In letting go of everything—including my identity—I became more like Jesus. Why? All because of the pressing and crushing of living missionally on foreign soil.

"No, Jesus. I wouldn't trade it," I said.

How much of my life had I spent avoiding the very thing that causes crazy growth? How long have I resisted this passage in James? "When all kinds of trials and temptations crowd into your lives my brothers, don't resent them as intruders, but welcome them as friends! Realise [*sic*] that they come to test your faith and to produce in you the quality of endurance. But let the process go on until that endurance is fully developed, and you will find you have become men of mature character with the right sort of independence" (James 1:2–4 PHILLIPS).

I don't often welcome trials and temptations as if they were my best friends. I certainly didn't overseas. Trials assaulted me like insipid intruders. But I'm learning to open my arms. Slowly I'm welcoming everything God sends, all the while studying other believers whose roots have gone deep, whose branches bear the fruit and flower of God's handiwork.

. . .

As I've pondered my journey and mined the pathways of Everything Christians—those who learned the secret of giving Him every part of their lives—I've realized something. Some folks grow while others stagnate. Why? What causes growthlessness? What, on the other hand, makes people more Jesusy—more like Him? My exploration of the *whys* behind that kind of radical change forms the framework of this book. The truths are hard-won from the soil of my life and the lives of others who thrive and love Jesus in this mixed-up world. George Barna delineates this exploration: "Some people reach the ultimate stages of wholeness and maturity within just a couple of decades while others failed to achieve such maturity after more than five decades of consistent religious activity and positive intent."[2]

What accounts for maturity, the hallmark of growth? Why do some languish while others thrive?

The questions remind me of the Israelites. God's heart for them was this: be set free from Egyptian tyranny, walk toward Jericho for a few weeks, then joyfully enter the promised land. But as they walked, they grumbled, disobeyed God, fashioned and worshipped a molten idol, and rebelled in all sorts of deceptive ways. Those few weeks turned into forty years, and even then only Joshua and Caleb were allowed to enter the land of milk and honey. Had they obeyed, they'd have reached the glory of new land in a handful of days, yet they wandered through the wilderness for years. And years.

I fear we are like those pesky Israelites. God wants to grow us up, to bring us to new vistas and promised lands aplenty. He created us for adventure, not ease. Instead of obeying in the moment and experiencing powerful spiritual growth, we wander around in circles chasing ease, trusting in ourselves to solve our problems, living a Godless life. We arrive forty years later, looking back, and wonder why in the world we didn't grow and why God seems terribly distant. In thinking about this book, I asked myself, *Why is it that some people can know Jesus for forty years and be stingy and untransformed? Why is it that others can exude Jesus four months after shaking hands with Him?*

Instead of obeying in the moment and experiencing powerful spiritual growth, we wander around in circles chasing ease, trusting in ourselves to solve our problems, living a Godless life.

The answer? It has to do with what those people do with everything. They either hoard their "everything" as a means to coddle and control their lives, or they joyfully relinquish everything to Jesus. And when that second group gives up everything, they gain Jesus, who is our everything.

I remember hearing a song as a kindergartener—a mournful song entitled "You Are Everything" by the Stylistics. There the singer tells his object of affection that she is his everything and everything is her. In other words, his entire world meant her. I cried when I heard that song, then I thought long and hard about it. (I was an introspective five-year-old.) Because of the circumstances of my childhood and feeling abandoned and abused, I longed for someone to become my everything. I looked for an "everything" in my parents, my stepparents, my friends, and neighborhood bullies. None of them became my everything. Quite the contrary. Often those whom I needed to be my everything ended up taking chunks of my soul with them, leaving me less-than.

I shrunk looking for my everything. Crumbled. Broke.

But at fifteen, when I heard about Jesus and His beautiful ways, I knew. He was the answer to my song-longing. He was the only One qualified to be my everything. And when He burst into my life, He became my everything.

Sometimes I forget, though, that He is everything, and everything is Him. I meander down me-first paths, hoping achievement or people or success will fill up every part of my heart. I chase unsatisfying ghosts, hints of fulfillment that dissipate the moment I reach them. I even despair, as I did in France. But Jesus keeps reminding me through His presence and His realness that He is everything. And I stumble back to Him.

I don't write this book as a condemnation or as a sermon. The last thing I want to do is to provide a "how to be the best Christian in ten easy steps" guide. I pen these words as a fellow struggler, as one who doesn't often feel Jesusy or strong or faith-filled. In this spiritual journey, I've come to see the importance of everything that's inside us, how we think, what our hearts tell us. If we are near to Jesus' mind and heart-beat, we will naturally act like Him. That's not a simple, catchy formula.

- What we think about God matters.
- How we allow Him to reign in our hearts matters.
- How we obey Him in the moment matters.

This book follows those three truths. We start with our heads, what we think about God. We'll move to our hearts, the place Jesus wants to revolutionize, to become our everything. And we'll end with our hands, how we live out Jesus' internal transformation.

Head. Heart. Hands. Giving every part of our lives—*everything*—to Jesus.

Care to journey alongside me toward an Everything life?

SECTION ONE

Head—What We Think

WHAT WE THINK ABOUT GOD, HIS WORLD, AND OURSELVES determines our growth story. If we have a low view of God, we will not go to Him for help or wisdom. If we overemphasize our depravity, we'll live in despair. If grace is the only aspect of God we embrace, we may veer toward a licentious lifestyle.

How can we truly know God's mind? Jesus said, "No one truly knows the Son except the Father, and no one truly knows the Father except the Son and those to whom the Son chooses to reveal him" (Luke 10:22 NLT). Jesus is our pathway to know God, to understand His ways. Jesus reveals God by the way He lived and the words He said. He gave the Holy Spirit to His followers to further reveal the Father.

In the following chapters we'll look at the mind, how we think, where we err, how God transforms our thinking. And in that exploration, it's my hope you'll experience wild freedom and new excitement in your adventure toward an everything life.

Chapter One

CULTIVATE THE DISCIPLINE OF ASTONISHMENT

> *This, after all, is the goal of the American dream: to make much of*
> *ourselves. But here the gospel and the American dream are clearly and*
> *ultimately antithetical to each other. While the goal of the American dream*
> *is to make much of us, the goal of the gospel is to make much of God.*
>
> —DAVID PLATT[1]

WHEN I SAT BENEATH THE EVERGREEN AT FIFTEEN YEARS OLD, the stars twinkled their brilliance above me. I felt the rough bark against my back while tears streaked my face. I heard the gospel in its entirety (if one can ever hear such magnificence in one perfect package), and I was stunned to silence. I was small, broken, haunted by swirling memories of the past. I lived as a fatherless daughter searching for the Daddy who would never leave me. Under the stars, the ground beneath me, God astonished me. His bigness. His sacrifice on the world's behalf. His ability to be everywhere, yet be concerned about me. His speaking things into existence from nothingness. I asked Him to please enter my life in the gentlest way. And He did.

When I think of Jesus-loving people, I venture back to this place of astonishment, this smallness of me compared to God's immensity. I run back to that place where my mind was overwhelmed by God's greatness. And I also think of others whose minds held big thoughts of God. I remember the people I met in Malaysia who couldn't bow low enough to worship God. I remember my friend Su, tears on her face becoming her petition. Oh, how she loved. I think of an unnamed man I met in Urbana, Illinois, who practically beamed Jesus, but who spoke of Him with reverence and awe. Paul in Ghana comes to mind, how his eyes dance when he tells the story of God providing for him in spectacular and mundane ways. Holly, dear Holly, who calls out of the blue because she hears a whisper from God and she must pass His encouragement on to me.

They see beyond the veil of this world while they grasp the upside-down kingdom where meek inherit and strong fall, while God reigns supreme overall.

In a world bent on human glory, folks like these stand out. They're the bewildering kind who think much of Jesus, yet decrease into obscurity like John the Baptist. They understand the proverb, "It is not good to eat much honey, nor is it glorious to seek one's own glory" (Prov. 25:27). They see beyond the veil of this world while they grasp the upside-down kingdom where meek inherit and strong fall, while God reigns supreme overall. I watch these people. I long to be like them, to think like them.

What does it mean to live in the discipline of astonishment? How can we deify God yet subvert our claim to deity? How can we embrace the cliché, God is God and I am not? The answer comes from theology, the way we think about God. When you read the word *theology*, you may yawn a bit, dismissing the term as boring, something relegated to banter in seminary halls. But theology is sexy; it's dynamic. And it's utterly important if we want Jesus to be our everything. In light of that, let's build a campfire around five truths.

TRUTH ONE: GOD CREATES

The triune God—Father, Son, Holy Spirit—created everything we see, touch, taste, perceive, and think. All things originate from Him. We see this clearly delineated in Scripture:

> *In the beginning the Word already existed.*
> *The Word was with God,*
> *and the Word was God.*
> *He existed in the beginning with God.*
> *God created everything through him,*
> *and nothing was created except through him.*
> *The Word gave life to everything that was created,*
> *and his life brought light to everyone.*
> *The light shines in the darkness,*
> *and the darkness can never extinguish it.* (John 1:1–5 NLT)

When the world careens out of control, we can rest in the fact that God spun this world with a simple word. Matter from emptiness. Beauty from void. Community from chaos.

Remembering God as Creator reminds us that God is in the growth business. He not only created trees, sky, air, and dirt, but He also matures them: "So neither he who plants nor he who waters is anything, but only God who gives the growth" (1 Cor. 3:7). I've spent a great deal of my Christian life trying to manufacture what only God can flourish. Although I have a choice to submit myself before the Creator of the world, to be humbly repentant, adopting a posture of learning, I cannot cause growth. I must depend on His ability to bring sprouts, limbs, flowers, and fruit.

TRUTH TWO: GOD IS *OTHER*

In college, as friends prayed for me to heal from the brokenness of the past, my heart bent toward revival. I read Leonard Ravenhill and listened to the late Keith Green. I prayed up a storm and read about great college prayer movements. And I discovered the book *The School of Christ* by T. Austin Sparks. In the first chapter he writes about the otherness of Christ.

I'd often thought about what those head-scratching disciples must've made of Jesus. He rarely responded the way they anticipated. His line of thinking confounded and confused them. Why? Because they tried to measure Christ by human standards. Christ was fully human, but paradoxically was also fully God, which made Him wildly unpredictable and downright strange.

Consider Sparks's words:

> The first thing [the disciples] learned was how other He was from themselves. They had to learn it. I do not think it came to them at the first moment. It was as they went on that they found themselves again and again clashing with His thoughts, His mind, His ways. They would urge Him to take a certain course, to do certain things, to go to certain places; they would seek to bring to bear upon Him their own judgments and their own feelings and their own ideas. But He would have none of it.[2]

How *other* Jesus is. How *other* God the Father is. How *other* the Holy Spirit is. Our triune, mysterious God is far above what we can think or perceive or categorize. Remember Isaiah's oft-quoted words:

> For my thoughts are not your thoughts,
>   neither are your ways my ways, declares the LORD.
> For as the heavens are higher than the earth,
>   so are my ways higher than your ways
>   and my thoughts than your thoughts. (Isa. 55:8–9)

And yet we falsely believe that we can manage just fine without Him. We cherish our uniqueness, our clever thoughts, forgetting that Wisdom and Power and Holiness personified empowers us. God as *other* is untamable, unmanageable, unpredictable. Which is why growth can be a frightening prospect.

Does your thinking fall far short of the otherness of God? I know mine does. I spend hours pondering issues, forgetting to consult God. I try to be the answer to my own prayers. I insulate myself, minimizing risk so I don't have to fling myself into the arms of this wild God.

I remember the funny song "Please Don't Send Me to Africa" from decades ago. I remember thinking, *This song resonates with me*. And yet, decades later, I found myself in Ghana, West Africa, with my then twelve-year-old son, Aidan, who dared to believe in God's otherness. He heard God tell him to dig wells, so he upheaved his comfortable sixth-grade life and followed Jesus' footsteps to Africa. There we met others who follow this strange, amazing God, and we were forever changed. As I type this, Aidan again stands on Ghanaian soil, following the beckoning of God that woos a now fifteen-year-old to that same continent.

God is other. We cannot explain Him. We cannot have perfect theology (though we value theology). We cannot attempt to know the mind of God fully. But as believers, we have an eternal resource, the Holy Spirit, who makes known to us God's intentions. When we consider the otherness of God, the overwhelming beauty and audacity of God to dwell within us can bring nothing but astonishment. The God who created, this otherly God, dares to stoop to such a place as our hearts.

> *We cherish our uniqueness, our clever thoughts, forgetting that Wisdom and Power and Holiness personified empowers us. God as other is untamable, unmanageable, unpredictable. Which is why growth can be a frightening prospect.*

Truth Three: God Redeems

My friend pushed against God, against me, against anyone who would dare speak truth in her life. She seemed to relish rebellion, yet all the while saying she believed in Jesus. For several years I puzzled over her words and her behavior, so much so that I had to place a boundary on our friendship. Years passed. One day I received a call from her. "I've met Jesus!" she said.

"What? I thought you were a Christian."

"No, I only thought I was," she said. I could hear the joy in her voice. "But I finally met Jesus, and I'll never be the same."

In that moment and in the subsequent years, I've seen radical redemption in my friend's life. Her words challenge me. Her life shouts Jesus. Her heart, oh, her heart, is so very beautiful. And when she e-mails or calls, instead of dreading her as I once did, I stop my day and hang on to her words.

God is a God who redeems. He beautifies even the most haggard. He rescues us from pits far too deep to scale. We, the helpless creation, must look to the only One who is able to free us. Consider how the following verses aptly sum up these first three aspects of God—the God who creates, who is other, who redeems:

> Christ is the visible image of the invisible God.
>> He existed before anything was created and is supreme over all
>> creation,
> for through him God created everything
>> in the heavenly realms and on earth.
> He made the things we can see
>> and the things we can't see—
> such as thrones, kingdoms, rulers, and authorities in the unseen world.
>> Everything was created through him and for him. [creates]
> He existed before anything else,
>> and he holds all creation together.

Christ is also the head of the church,
*   which is his body.*
He is the beginning,
*   supreme over all who rise from the dead.*
*   So he is first in everything.* [other]
For God in all his fullness
*   was pleased to live in Christ,*
and through him God reconciled everything to himself.
He made peace with everything in heaven and on earth
*   by means of Christ's blood on the cross.* [redeems] (Col. 1:15–20 NLT)

We cannot fully satisfy a holy God. Our redemption is an outrageous, initiating act accomplished by God alone. He pursued humanity to such an extent that His feet landed on earth, and He chased after us until He rescued us at the cross. We did not climb onto those wooden beams. We could not receive the nails that pierced those holy hands. We who are not kingly wore no thorn crown. We could not drink the cup of God's wrath. "For while we were still helpless, at the right time Christ died for the ungodly" (Rom. 5:6 NASB). God did what we could not. He sent His beautifully sinless Son to take our place, to satisfy for all time God's wrath upon sin: "For our sake he made him to be sin who knew no sin, so that in him we might become the righteousness of God" (2 Cor. 5:21).

God transforms. He who creates, He who thinks otherworldly thoughts, dares to redeem an obstinate world. If we camp in that place, remembering the gift we could never, ever pay back, we will live astonished lives, and our growth will be the best kind—the kind that emerges from gratitude, from thinking rightly about God.

TRUTH FOUR: GOD SEES

When I traveled to Ghana, my son Aidan and I were part of a team that had already been assembled from another local church. Though

I'm sure none of the members meant to exclude me, the nature of the trip and our addition later made it hard for me to fit in. As I stepped onto Ghanaian soil, I prayed, "Lord, help me know that You see me here." I made a determination to be small, unnoticed. No longer an author or a speaker, I spent my time behind the scenes. But loneliness settled inside me like untreated malaria. I cried out to God from this small, small place.

God's answer came late one night during a van ride over rough roads where sleeping sheep and goats served as living obstacles. I sat next to my new Ghanaian friend Paul and asked for his story. He shared his heart, how he walked with Jesus, how he met his wife, how he struggled to know whether he'd have another meal. I felt privileged to hear his words. I shared my heart in exchange. Then he said something that helped me know God sees. He told me my empathy encouraged him to share his story. I realized then that I had played a role in my trek to Ghana. To listen. And to hear an amazing story— proof that God saw me and would reward my smallness.

Hagar, maidservant of Sarai, had an encounter with God when she despaired of life, when her smallness bordered on despair. After Sarai mistreated her, she fled to the wilderness and sat down by a spring. An angel of the Lord appeared to her and encouraged her. She would have a son, and she was to name him Ishmael. He'd be "a wild donkey of a man," and she would live to see him grow up. After that encounter, she named God *El Roi*, the God who sees: "She gave this name to the LORD who spoke to her: 'You are the God who sees me,' for she said, 'I have now seen the One who sees me.' That is why the well was called Beer Lahai Roi; it is still there, between Kadesh and Bered" (Gen. 16:7–14 NIV). *Beer Lahai Roi* means "the well of the living one who sees me" (NASB).

We forget, don't we? We place God in our small boxes, limiting Him to humanness, forgetting His omnipresence. He is everywhere. He is everything. Of course He sees. He not only sees the entire world and universe, but His vision becomes myopic too. He can focus on one of us at a time, even if we travel far away from home and comfort. He can encourage in us-shaped ways and sends folks our way to prove He is good and He sees our needs.

Psalm 8:3–5 reminds us of our seeing God. The first few verses of the Davidic psalm speak of God's greatness and majesty, His power over creation. Then we read this glorious insertion:

> *When I look at the night sky and see the work of your fingers—*
> *the moon and the stars you set in place—*
> *what are mere mortals that you should think about them,*
> *human beings that you should care for them?*
> *Yet you made them only a little lower than God*
> *and crowned them with glory and honor.* (NLT)

We are small. He is big. And yet He sees. That should spur us toward crazy growth, rugged trust, and reverential awe.

TRUTH FIVE: GOD INHABITS

Our daughter Julia heard demonic voices when we lived in France. For several months we puzzled over her behavior, thinking she simply had a hard time adjusting to the culture and language. But eventually she broke down and told us she heard awful voices telling her to be disobedient to us and mean to her siblings. At night the voices tormented her, woke her up. We prayed for her. We told her about Jesus, but she couldn't seem to grasp Him or even reach for Him. A few weeks later some friends from the States came to watch our kids while we went to a leadership summit in Lisbon, Portugal. We pulled them aside and told them about Julia and the voices. They promised to pray for her and be extra sensitive to her while we were away.

During the conference we received a voice message. Julia's little voice piped through saying, "Mommy and Daddy? I just want to let you know that I asked Jesus to come into my heart." I could hear the joy in her voice, but inwardly I feared. Would she still be tormented?

When we came home, I asked her how she was doing: "Are you hearing those voices?"

"Well," she said. "I do hear a voice, but it tells me to make right choices."

"That's the Holy Spirit," I told her. In the moment she met Jesus, He replaced the demonic voices with His Spirit. He truly lived inside our daughter.[3] A few weeks later she asked to be baptized in the Mediterranean Sea. The pictures are framed above her bed.

Seeing His brilliance and power, understanding His ability to create, realizing His might, contrast wildly with the truth that this God, this amazing God, inhabits us.

God is present. And if we have given our lives to Him, He, as Holy Spirit, resides in us. He makes His home inside our lives. Seeing His brilliance and power, understanding His ability to create, realizing His might, contrast wildly with the truth that this God, this amazing God, inhabits us. Because of this, we who want to grow need to remind ourselves of His constant, abiding presence. Like Brother Lawrence, the monk who joyfully washed dishes with Jesus beside Him, we can practice His presence every single moment.

In my frenetic pace of life, I've forgotten His presence. It's a choice in those times to cry out to the God who lives within me, asking Him to lift my head. This beautiful, inhabiting God breathes encouragement into me, reminding me that I am His child, worthy of His sacrifice. I don't need to wallow in a place of stress because He understands. He is Emmanuel, God with us, and He sees us—an astonishing fact. Simply meditating there will change our growth patterns forever.

• • •

It is a discipline to think astonished. Often we are bewildered by the details of our lives, forgetting about the bigness of the God we serve. He made everything. He is utterly other. Yet He chose to redeem us. He sees us. And if we are His followers, He lives within us. We are simply His followers, dependent on Him for new life. The author of Hebrews summed up our need for astonishment: "Let us be grateful for receiving a kingdom that cannot be shaken, and thus let us offer to God acceptable worship, with reverence and awe, for our God is a consuming fire" (Heb. 12:28–29). May our thoughts be consumed with our awe-worthy God. And may those thoughts translate into astonishment-based living, where we live to make much of God and less of us. That is the heart of the gospel, after all—the six-letter word that should change our thinking forever.

Questions for Reflection and Discussion

- *How does knowing God created everything from nothing influence your behavior? Or does it? Why or why not?*

- *What aspect of the otherness of God do you find hard to grasp? How do you act in an "otherly" way most days?*

- *Looking back over the past four months, what parts of your life has God redeemed?*

- *How does realizing God sees you right now help you cope with your current circumstances? Or does it raise more questions?*

- *When was the last time you truly felt the Holy Spirit living in and through you? What were the circumstances in your life during that time?*

LIVE THE SIX-LETTER WORD THAT CHANGES EVERYTHING

I am not ashamed of the gospel, because it is the power of God for the salvation of everyone who believes: first for the Jew, then for the Gentile.

—ROMANS 1:16 NIV

AT CAMP SAMBICA ON THE SHORES OF LAKE SAMMAMISH, we college students trained ourselves to share the gospel, the six-letter word that changes everything. We used the five fingers of our hands to communicate this truth to children and young teens.

Finger one was our thumb pointing back to us. Positioned there, we said, "We are all sinners."

We added the pointer finger and pointed a gun. "The penalty for sin is death."

We adhered our middle finger to our pointer, then pointed those two fingers heavenward while our thumb jutted out earthward. "God sent Jesus to come to earth from heaven as God in the flesh, living a sinless life."

We added the ring finger, then stretched out our arms wide, using both hands, pinkie fingers tucked away until our bodies formed a cross. "Jesus died on the cross and paid the penalty for our sins."

The last bit involved isolating that pinkie finger, wee little finger number five, and pointing it to the sky. "Jesus rose again and will return too."

In essence, that is the gospel, the good news. We were a big, fat mess, but God remedied that mess by dressing in skin, living a perfect life, and becoming the sacrifice we could never be, the exclamation point being the raucous resurrection. Five fingers. Five truths. Simple, right?

Paul defined the gospel in similar terms:

> Now I would remind you, brothers, of the gospel I preached to you, which you received, in which you stand, and by which you are being saved, if you hold fast to the word I preached to you—unless you believed in vain. For I delivered to you as of first importance what I also received: that Christ died for our sins in accordance with the Scriptures, that he was buried, that he was raised on the third day in accordance with the Scriptures, and that he appeared to Cephas, then to the twelve. (1 Cor. 15:1–5)

We were a big, fat mess, but God remedied that mess by dressing in skin, living a perfect life, and becoming the sacrifice we could never be, the exclamation point being the raucous resurrection.

The gospel of Jesus Christ should be both simple and profound. Simple in its beauty, but profound in the life change it should bring. No longer enslaved to sin, which so easily entangles, we receive a new nature from the Spirit of God. We are to live like Christ—self-sacrificing, loving to a fault, humble, empowered, fully alive. We now represent God's kingdom in this earthly realm, clearly establishing Jesus as our King and God's rule as supreme over all. The gospel is about spreading and living

God's fame. Even Daniel, in exile, understood that God's actions on this earth were not for our benefit, but for His glory alone. He wrote, "O Lord, hear; O Lord, forgive. O Lord, pay attention and act. Delay not, for your own sake, O my God, because your city and your people are called by your name" (Dan. 9:19).

Unfortunately we've settled for thinking with a watered-down perspective. We'd rather determine the minimum amount of work, viewing Christianity as a pass/fail class with a benevolent, easygoing teacher. We pick and choose the tenets of the gospel we personally like (Jesus dying for us), but disregard the calling of Christ (He asks us to die too). Kyle Idleman, who wrote *Not a Fan*, asks an important question: "Has the Church done a sort of bait-and-switch with people, selling the Jesus life that's easy and comfortable, or do you think people have chosen the things they want to apply?"[1] We love all the love, but we shrink back when we're called to love our enemies. We love the grace, but when we have to extend it to a perpetrator, we cringe. We love Jesus' unselfish sacrifice on our behalf, but we'd prefer that others serve us, doing everything we'd love for them to do.

The gospel isn't a life management program. It shouldn't merely be the crutch we fall on when life gets ugly. It should be the legs we walk on, the air we breathe.

The gospel isn't a life management program. It shouldn't merely be the crutch we fall on when life gets ugly. It should be the legs we walk on, the air we breathe. When I read the book of Acts, I'm humbled and a little scared too. Why? Because I don't resemble those folks. I certainly don't think like them. My inner transformation hasn't looked so dynamic, so entirely world-changing. I haven't willingly suffered for the sake of the gospel. I haven't counted all things loss. I haven't given Jesus everything. Instead I cling to my possessions, relish my comfort, and spend a great deal of time seeking earthly peace.

When I stop and consider Jesus on that cross, though, I reorient myself to this radical, life-altering call. In thinking about His death, I realize the call to follow Him cannot be easy because following leads to death. I can't turn away from His thorn-poked brow, the blood running earthward, hands pegged to a rough-hewn beam, His cries of forgiveness even then. It's there, at the base of the cross, that I understand afresh why those crazy apostles suffered much for Jesus, why they counted their lives as nothing in light of sharing the gospel with others.

The gospel they shared was simple, but it earthquaked the foundations of people's lives. It called for allegiance, total adherence, but it promised the Holy Spirit, the One who would empower them to live out that kind of commitment. Unfortunately, the gospel we hear most often in our pulpits or even friend-to-friend looks nothing like this. It sounds more like platitudes and self-help manuals:

- Meet Jesus and your life will improve.
- Jesus will save your marriage! Your kids! Your life!
- Jesus and His grace will forgive you of all that awful stuff you did. Now you have a clean slate and can live the best life you can imagine!

It's not that these things aren't true—to some extent they are—but they are wholly incomplete. We don't preach (or live) the whole gospel. Instead we live the AYDI gospel, the All You Do Is gospel.

When we share Christ, we often present the reality of the Christian life in manageable bites, starting with All You Do Is. We woo people along with the least amount of commitment, only to add more requirements the longer they walk with Christ. The progression looks a lot like this:

- All you do is say this simple sinner's prayer.
- All you do is attend church.

- All you do is stop doing bad things.
- All you do is read your Bible.
- All you do is get baptized.
- All you do is learn how to pray.
- All you do is memorize scriptures.
- All you do is learn how to share your faith.
- All you do is attend Bible studies.
- All you do is teach a Bible study.
- All you do is raise your kids to be Christians.
- All you do is make sure your marriage reflects Jesus.
- All you do is go on a short-term mission trip.
- All you do is give money to the church.
- All you do is give money to those in need.
- All you do is become a pastor or a missionary or a deacon or an elder.
- All you do is die to your own desires and embrace Jesus' lordship.[2]

This progression is not the gospel. Where it ends, "All you do is die to your own desires and embrace Jesus' lordship," is where it should start. As Western Christians, we tend to think linearly, but the gospel is more circular, all-encompassing. The gospel isn't a progressive list of improvement tactics. We do others (and ourselves) a disservice if we believe it is. If we assign a stairway of steps starting with a simple prayer and ending with lordship, we invite confusion and disillusionment. What happens when all the pretty things we share about the gospel seem untrue because reality interrupts? We live in Jesus' parable of the sower, rootless: "The seed on the rocky soil represents those who hear the message and immediately receive it with joy. But since they don't have deep roots, they don't last long. They fall away as soon as they have problems or are persecuted for believing God's word" (Matt. 13:20–21 NLT).

We wonder why our kids, after living in the nurture of a Christian home, fall away once they're in the big, bad world. Perhaps it's because we haven't shared the whole gospel. Idleman confirms this phenomenon: "What I see happen with a lot of our college students is that they get out, they experience some suffering, they go through some difficulties and they're no longer fans of Jesus. They were fans when everything was good, but suddenly their faith is challenged in one way or another, and [that] didn't match up with the faith they were presented with, with the Gospel they were taught."[3]

The gospel is not AYDI. It should be "all your life is the gospel."

Ironically our nickname for our fifteen-year-old son is Aydi. Yet he doesn't represent that kind of watered-down gospel at all. As I mentioned earlier, this summer Aidan traveled again to Ghana, this time to the capital. While he was there, the leader asked my son to share with the full team. He spoke of hardship, about Jesus helping us through difficulties, and he cried when he recounted some of my difficulties growing up. His heart in that moment was to help other kids on his team with family issues. Once he opened up, others did, ushering in a two-hour prayer time. Of course I'm proud of my son, but the point is that most fifteen-year-old boys don't act this way. Unless they've been captured by the gospel and utterly transformed. No program made my son stand up and minister to people. No list made him concerned about people half a world away. Jesus did that. His call did that. Perhaps we should abandon AYDI Christianity and instead humbly follow Jesus as my son Aidan does, letting go of his comfort and daring to follow Jesus wherever He leads.

We live and breathe and follow a paradoxical gospel. We're to equate success not with the world's success, but with our ability to die to our desires. This echoes John 12:24: "I tell you the truth, unless a kernel of wheat falls to the ground and dies, it remains only a single seed. But if it dies, it produces many seeds" (NIV). We who want to hold on to our control have a hard time with words like these.

We don't much like death. We'd rather produce seeds another way. But death to ourselves, our agendas, our expectations, our hopes is necessary to find the deep joy that comes when we fully relinquish ourselves to the gospel.

. . .

When I reread the book of Acts, this mind-set of joy rocks me. Folks willingly gave themselves up for service. With smiles, they gave away their stuff. They sang in prison, rejoiced in trials, and traveled to difficult places with praise on their lips. Where the AYDI gospel is measured and safe and vanilla, the real gospel is unmeasured, unsafe, and utterly flavorful. If we live in its tenets, giving up our wills, our agendas, our fears, our everything, we will experience surprising joy, the deepest sort of joy that comes from obedience. I don't know about you, but I don't want to live a vanilla life. I don't think Aidan does either. We want to live a life where we crave the things of God, hunger for righteousness, and worry more about what God thinks of our reputations than what others think. We are an unholy people in need of a holy gospel. When we come to Jesus, we come unclean, but this dirty state serves as a catalyst for a new life, a hunger for a life that counts. This kind of life, where death reigns in us, produces deep, abiding growth.

We want to live a life where we crave the things of God, hunger for righteousness, and worry more about what God thinks of our reputations than what others think.

All you do is this: lay down your life.

QUESTIONS FOR REFLECTION
AND DISCUSSION

- *What is the gospel? And how does your life today reflect it?*

- *Have you ever heard the gospel presented as All You Do Is . . . ? Or have you thought of it that way? If so, how has that view of the gospel brought disillusionment?*

- *How do people water down the gospel? How do you?*

- *What does it mean to live the gospel? How would your life look if you truly laid down your life for Jesus and gave Him everything?*

- *Who in your life emanates the gospel? What about that person intrigues or draws you?*

Chapter Three

Discern the Vow Factor

Life is a series of promises we break or make to ourselves.

—Mary DeMuth

I STEP ON THE SCALE, READ THE NUMBER, AND GRIMACE. Then I vow. Next morning, up bright with the sun, I tie my running shoes, grab the leash and my faithful golden retriever, and jog down the road, fulfilling my little vow to lose my middle-age weight.

My son grabs my hand and the hand of his sister, then asks, "Can I pray tonight?" Our family bows in unison at the burger joint, and fifteen-year-old Aidan prays his heart out, asking God to save the 4.5 billion people who have yet to believe in Jesus. I nearly cry. I vow to pray more for this lost world. So I do, but then life helps me forget.

A memory flashes back. I was alone, walking home from school at a quickened pace, always worried that killers would grab me. I unlocked the back door of my home, then shut it behind me, jimmying the lock shut again. My heart thumped as I waited for my grandmother's call. She asked about my day, calmed me down. In that recollection of thought, I vow to be there for my kids, to be home when they're home. In many ways I've succeeded in that vow, though I'm not always as emotionally present as I should be.

What is a vow? A vow is simply a promise we make, often to ourselves, but also to God and others. Biblically we can justify this practice. The hairy Nazirites who didn't drink a lick of alcohol made vows to be separate. Hannah, Samuel's mother, made a vow that she'd give her child up to the service of the Lord if she ever had a child. In the New Testament, Jesus spoke of vows as well when He said our yeses should be yeses and our noes should be noes (Matt. 5:33–37).

On first glance, vow making seems the ideal solution to growth, right? It feels like a fruit of the Spirit on steroids, this bent toward self-control. It's flattering to our bootstrapping ways. And we can certainly justify a vow that sounds holy. In my book *Building the Christian Family You Never Had*, I tackled this issue of vow making for the pioneer parent. I wrote, "Vows can be a stimulus for positive change when the vow aligns with the pattern God is establishing in our lives. But a vow that is made to calm our fears, to bolster our confidence, to justify our anger, or to take upon ourselves the work that is really God's area of responsibility is a vow that will cause frustration and lead to defeat."[1]

We make all sorts of vows without even knowing it. Vows begin in our heads, then live on in our actions. Here are some common ones. Note that some of these are conscious; others are unconscious. Some are positive; others are destructive. Some deal directly with Christianity, while others are internal, emotional vows. Do you see yourself in any of these?

- I will read through the Bible in a year.
- I will protect my heart from injury by closing myself off from others.
- I will no longer overeat.
- I will never forgive what he did to me.
- I will not parent the way I was parented.

- I will do everything I can to justify my existence on earth.
- I will attend church every time the doors are open.
- I will never trust anyone. Ever.
- I will earn her love.
- I will do anything to be financially successful.
- I won't cheat on my spouse.
- I will control my emotions.
- I will always look holy to others.
- I will succeed at any cost.
- I will do whatever it takes to get people to like me.
- I will be a servant, choosing to be overlooked.
- I will sacrifice my personality by always doing what another person wants me to do.
- I will write in a prayer journal.
- I will never grow up.
- I will join an accountability group.

Usually a destructive personal vow results from an injury. One of mine was, *I will do everything I can to justify my existence on earth.* Growing up, I had a hard time believing my family loved me. Of course, part of this was my fault. Because of my insatiable need for love (I hadn't yet met Jesus), I placed high expectations on the adults in my life to fill every nook and cranny of my heart. When I failed, folks in my family not only withdrew but also shamed me, sometimes even ridiculing me for my failure. When this happened, I'd think something like, *If I fail, I'm rejected. So if I'm perfect, I'll prove to them that I am worthy of love.* Using this simple logic, I lived a lifelong vow to overwork, overimpress, overachieve.

Oddly, though, this didn't work a lick! Half the time folks closest to me didn't even notice my achievements, and the rejection continued even when I succeeded. Although I achieved more than I failed, it didn't seem to matter because the rejection felt bigger in my heart.

Eventually I must've realized that this pursuit of achievement wouldn't merit affection, but it would herald a strong sense of satisfaction. If I couldn't earn love, then at least I could impress myself and others outside my family with my accomplishments. Achieving became my drug, my recognition, my insatiable need.

This vow continues to plague me. It strangles my growth. It mars the way I view God. Although intellectually I know that God loves me desperately, I still picture Him shaking His holy head in heaven, tsk-tsk-tsking me when I fail. And when I "win" at something, I'm far too busy thinking of the next thing to achieve to really stop and rejoice in the moment. Nothing I do is ever enough. Which proves why vows can be problematic to the Christian who wants to be like Jesus.

Why is that?

Simply this: a vow is something we think in our own strength. It's an internal determination to fix our lives without God's help. It's looking to our own pluck and gumption to achieve what the Holy Spirit wants to achieve in our lives. It is being self-led, not Spirit-led. And anything that smacks of a self-led life will ultimately fail. God doesn't call us to bootstrap. He calls us to take off our boots because we stand on holy ground before Him. He beckons us to let Him control the outcome of our walk instead of us trying to manage spiritual growth on our own. When we live under the heaviness of the yoke of vows, we fall prey to campaign Christianity, where everything becomes some sort of self-controlling campaign to better ourselves.

> *God doesn't call us to bootstrap. He calls us to take off our boots because we stand on holy ground before Him.*

We forget so easily these Jesus words: "Remain in me, and I will remain in you. For a branch cannot produce fruit if it is severed from the vine, and you cannot be fruitful unless you remain in me. Yes, I am the vine; you are the branches. Those who remain in me, and I in them, will produce much fruit. For apart from me you can do nothing" (John 15:4–5 NLT).

Stop right now.

Reread that last sentence: "For apart from me you can do nothing." Nothing. Sobering, isn't it?

We must ask ourselves why certain vows hurt our growth. Here are three ways.

1. We Forget That Our Strength Can Never Mimic God's

We who love control, who may be well meaning when we make vows, are sometimes guilty of accomplishing little for the kingdom of God because we're too concerned about creating our own kingdoms. As I write this, I shiver a bit. I wonder how much of my Christian life has become trying to do things in my own wimpy strength. Of thinking I can live the Christian life just fine on my own. Of worrying about what this untamed, holy God would demand of me, so I take care of my daily living without His input. Of making vows to protect myself when that is clearly not my job, nor am I very good at it. Of creating my own spiritual list, not even bothering to consult the One who made me.

I had a friend in college who hinted at this problem in my life through her own disclosure. I poured out my heart, the frustration with my level of growth. She said something like, "Mary, I've learned the hard way that when I try to control my relationship with God, telling Him where I want to grow and how I would like to accomplish that, I strangle Him from truly working on my behalf. When I let Him be in control of how He wants to grow me is when I truly grow."

Paul echoed my friend's words when he wrote, "Do not stifle the Holy Spirit" (1 Thess. 5:19 NLT). He instructed us not to grieve the Spirit: "Do not bring sorrow to God's Holy Spirit by the way you live.

Remember, he has identified you as his own, guaranteeing that you will be saved on the day of redemption" (Eph. 4:30 NLT). What stifles, grieves, and brings sorrow to the Holy Spirit? It's our seeming capability to live our lives apart from Him. We think we can manage on our own, so we reject the help that God readily supplies. We fear that if we let Him be in control, He'll make us open up to people, risk ourselves, do scary things, or let go of the sins we cherish.

2. WE EXPERIENCE DEFEAT WHEN WE LEAD OUR LIVES

Yet Paul further gave us the cure to a self-willed life: "Since we are living by the Spirit, let us follow the Spirit's leading in every part of our lives" (Gal. 5:25 NLT). I can't read that verse without seeing how very little I keep my ears tuned in to His voice. Sure, I pray before meals. I try to have an ongoing dialogue with Jesus throughout my days, but often I'm living in la-la land, on some sort of strange Mary-fueled autopilot, acting and reacting in neutral. This is not the Everything life God envisions for us. He wants all of us, all the time, our minds and hearts deeply engaged with His so we will joyfully follow Him toward every single adventure He plans for us. This is not me vowing to be a good girl or me planning to be holy. This is me (and you) daring to follow the leading of the Holy Spirit of God.

He wants all of us, all the time, our minds and hearts deeply engaged with His so we will joyfully follow Him toward every single adventure He plans for us.

In that pursuit, He settles our worth issues. Often our vows stem from past injury. We dutifully obey our vows to fill a void in our hearts. But when we chase after God and His pursuits, He strangely and beautifully shows us our worth. He fills us. In that, we heal, and we find our little vows to be insufficient and somewhat silly.

One night around the dinner table when we were sharing our highs and lows of the day, I struggled with what I would say. I've always felt it important for parents to model genuine authenticity with their kids, but that night I didn't want to lay my heart out there. The kids shared highs and lows, my husband too. Finally, all eyes on me, with food and joy between us, I took a deep breath. "I have mainly a low today," I said. "I got a rejection from a publisher," I told my family. I shared how I grew up always feeling that I had to achieve to justify the space I took up on earth, so when I got rejected, it put me in a very bad place, feeling like I didn't belong here or I didn't have worth. One by one my sweet children, and then my husband, shared why they were glad I lived on this crazy earth. Their words eased my pain, helped me see my worth wasn't tied to an external entity wanting to publish me. It wasn't connected to me being liked by the cool people. I was worthy because God made me uniquely me. That's who my kids and husband loved. Not some automaton who could slash her to-do list in a single bound. Not Wonder Woman who fulfilled every vow to achieve. They loved me, the woman who failed yet loved Jesus and loved them.

Funny how simple life becomes when we pare it down to that central truth Jesus taught His disciples. Love God. Love others. All other vows pale by comparison.

3. We Self-Protect Rather Than Worship God

When we vow to live our lives a certain way, we subtract God from the equation of our lives. And when we vow to protect ourselves, we rob God of His job. He created our hearts, our lives, our wants, our hopes. He is best capable to fulfill them. Often I've made a vow to protect my heart at any cost. Though I've tried to discard that vow, much of it lingers. I have a hard time risking in new relationships. I don't pursue like I should. I hold back. I stay on the periphery of life, afraid of deep engagement.

When we vow to live our lives a certain way, we subtract God from the equation of our lives. And when we vow to protect ourselves, we rob God of His job.

After being injured in relationships again and again, I no longer want to risk such heartache. I like safe people.

But as I've processed my healing, I've realized security and relational safety have become an idol. I worship peace and harmony, forgetting that kingdom work is messied with relationships that don't always work out the way we want them to. Jesus often calls us to risk. He asks us to be vulnerable, to be authentic, so others can see Him in and through us. If I continue to worship the idol of self-protection, I'll never grow in my relationships. I'll not venture out to people in the margins of life. I'll settle for sanitized friendships. I'll back away from conflict. I'll keep holed up in my house, preferring the safety of my little family to the big, bad world outside my front door.

God calls us to shed the vow of protecting our hearts. He's asking us to trust Him with our lives, our relationships, our fears. We aren't to be in control of every single thing. To do so is to insult the Creator of the universe. When we try to manage our lives without Him, we become god at the helm.

. . .

Although it's not wrong to live self-controlled lives in terms of celebrating discipline and working hard, we will not be able to sustain our Christian lives if we live them entirely in our own strength. When we campaign like this, repeatedly making New Year's resolutions, we become the managers of our growth. Growth comes from God, to those with surrendered, yielded hearts. Living in our own strength cannot grow us in the long term. Nor should we want it to. We're all pretty tired, aren't we? Tired of doing it all. Tired of failing. Tired of keeping people at a distance. Tired of trying to achieve so others will notice. Tired of people's opinions of us. In that desperate fatigue and the consequent defeat that comes with it, Jesus waits for us, arms wide open, heart fully alive, ready to receive us to Himself. He beckons us to rest in His embrace, to be freed from our fears, and to lay our vows at His feet.

He requires only that our love be ardent for Him and our hearts be willing to love others in the same way. Simple as that.

> *Although it's not wrong to live self-controlled lives in terms of celebrating discipline and working hard, we will not be able to sustain our Christian lives if we live them entirely in our own strength.*

QUESTIONS FOR REFLECTION AND DISCUSSION

- *Which vows on the list resonated with you? What vows have you created over the course of your life?*

- *In the past year, when have you lived in your own strength? What happened in your life as a result? And when have you lived in God's strength? How did your attitude differ?*

- *What does self-protection look like in your life?*

- *What's the difference between having self-control and controlling your life without God's help?*

- *Ask a friend, "What do you think is one of my vows?" Or ask, "How do you see me living my life in reaction to my past?"*

Let Go of the Giants

Obviously, I'm not trying to win the approval of people, but of God.
If pleasing people were my goal, I would not be Christ's servant.

—Galatians 1:10 NLT

I CAN'T LET GO OF FRIENDS VERY WELL, PARTICULARLY ones where conflict is left unsaid and I have no idea why we've veered away from each other. My first instinct is to pester, cajole, or investigate why things went wrong. This is pathology for me, as I still can't shake a friend from years and years ago whom I offended. She sent back every letter I'd ever written her, and that was that. Yet she still takes up emotional space in my mind. She looms large there, reminding me of my failure.

I realize that my way of viewing people and my desire to control relationships are unhealthy and sinful. Yet I'm growing. When we dropped off our eldest at college for her freshman year—far away from my control—I kept thinking I'd burst with sadness as we traversed the campus, unpacked her things, gave her wings. But I burst the other way, with joy—proof that God moves my heart in the right direction. I can learn to let go.

Simply put, when we think of other people as our center and fulfillment, we live frustrated lives. Constantly disappointed, some of us use this as a reason to control people, only to find that most eventually find a way to rebel against our desires. Some, like me, value others' opinions so much that if they turn on us, we despair, feeling abandoned. But to become more like Jesus we must understand that the only growth we can be in charge of is our own. We can't make people grow. True growth involves the activity of the Holy Spirit and an act of someone else's will. But we can lead Holy Spirit–enticing lives that produce in others a longing to change. It's all about our mind-set, freeing others in our minds to blessedly be themselves and determining to trust fully in Jesus for our strength and joy.

> *Simply put, when we think of other people as our center and fulfillment, we live frustrated lives.*

Think about the unchangeable I Am. He never changes, but the people of earth do. They move, leave, grow, disrespect, smother. Heartbroken, God watches His prodigals walk away, yet He lets us wander, not violating free will. Why don't we grant that same kind of freedom to people in our lives? Why must we cling to those who walk away instead of granting freedom? We must give the same liberty God gives to prodigals—an ability to let them go—or we'll be perennially bound to others for our happiness and effective service. We partner with God (and grow) when we understand the heartbeat of heartbreak—the more we love, the more it hurts, and the more we have to let go. In that painful space, we have a choice: punish those who hurt us through control, or lay our hurt at the feet of the One who understands. Our task shouldn't be punishing the villains in our lives, but enlarging the God who heals us from all wounds. Our growth comes from relinquishing our friends and family into His capable arms and fighting the urge to control others.

How can we grow through the difficult relationships God places in our lives? How should we think of them?

LET GOD CONVICT

Why do people change? Because they want to. Because they're inspired by the Holy Spirit to do so. Not because they're coerced, guilted, or forced.

I remember a story my friend George told me several years ago. He shared Christ with a guy on his college campus. The student heard the message, realized it was true, and gave his heart to Jesus. At the time the guy lived with his girlfriend. Later, one of George's friends asked him, "Don't you think you need to tell him that he shouldn't sleep with his girlfriend?"

Our task shouldn't be punishing the villains in our lives, but enlarging the God who heals us from all wounds.

George said no, which shocked the questioner. "If I tell him to do that, he will forever need me to be the Holy Spirit to him. That's not going to provide lasting conviction or growth. Better to let the Holy Spirit change him from the inside out."

Several weeks later, George heard a knock on his door late at night. It was his newly converted friend, sleeping bag tucked under his arm. "I was just reading in the Bible about fornication, and I realized I was guilty of it. I have nowhere else to stay but my girlfriend's place. Can I stay here?" George's patience and trust in God to convict changed this man's life. Madame Guyon, a French mystic from the eighteenth century, concured, "It is in vain for man to endeavor to instruct man in those things which the Holy Spirit alone can teach."[1]

In similar fashion, I learned recently of someone's unethical business practices. The more I heard, the more unsettled I became. I asked the Lord for clarity about this issue, and although it grieved me deeply, I didn't sense His call to confront. Later that day, I read this scripture:

"Do not contend with a man for no reason, when he has done you no harm" (Prov. 3:30). I could pray for him, but for me to confront him about secondhand information would not have been wise.

BECOME DISPASSIONATE

One ancient school of thought involved detachment, becoming dispassionate about others whose lives negatively affected ours. In early church history, they called this *apatheia*. Not the same as apathy, it was a deliberate disconnection from people for the sake of being able to thrive when relationships were painful.

I could've used this school of thought in college and early marriage. When my relationships went sour or pain came my way through the hand of another, I atrophied. I couldn't move, think, work, or do anything. I'd become so enmeshed in the pain of others that I couldn't navigate my life. I see this in some parents when they can't let go of their children as they enter adulthood. I receive prayer requests for thirty-eight-year-old sons from anguished parents who still fill that parenting role. Our task on this earth isn't to fret over everyone, allowing others' choices to dictate our moods; it's to seek hard the favor of God, to let Him be our everything. If we base our worth on the success of those we love, we will constantly live on a false and teetering edge of security. Other people can't throw us into depression. We have the choice to exercise *apatheia*, to disconnect for the sake of prayer and our health.

> *If we base our worth on the success of those we love, we will constantly live on a false and teetering edge of security.*

Persecution also comes at the hands of others. Paul asserted, "All who desire to live a godly life in Christ Jesus will be persecuted" (2 Tim. 3:12). It's an inevitability. Those who pursue Christ passionately will tick off the powers of darkness that will then incite people against us. If we are fully tied to their opinions for us to move forward in our work, we will quit. Paul endured extreme persecution, often at the hands of fellow countrymen, and sometimes from people into whom he had poured his life. But as I read his epistles, he didn't spend an inordinate amount of time directly addressing those folks. He pointed them out as cautionary tales, but he didn't seem to spend emotional energy on them. If he had, he most likely wouldn't have taken the second and third missionary journeys.

SUBORDINATE OTHER RELATIONSHIPS

Sometimes I cringe when I read Jesus' words. Do you? He said some pretty harsh things about our closest relationships. Peter felt the weight of this as he left everyone behind to follow Jesus. He said to Jesus, "We've left our homes to follow you."

"Yes," Jesus replied, "and I assure you that everyone who has given up house or wife or brothers or parents or children, for the sake of the Kingdom of God, will be repaid many times over in this life, and will have eternal life in the world to come" (Luke 18:28–30 NLT). Jesus asks us for everything and everyone. We are not called to follow half-heartedly. We can't bury our dead, coddle our mothers, or place anyone above His kingly rule.

Earlier in Luke, Jesus spelled it out plainly. "If you want to be my disciple, you must hate everyone else by comparison—your father and mother, wife and children, brothers and sisters—yes, even your own life. Otherwise, you cannot be my disciple" (Luke 14:26 NLT). Note the word *cannot*. If we want to be disciples of Jesus Christ, our devotion to Him must be supreme over our devotion to others. When Jesus simplified growth by telling us to love God and love others, the order of His statements can't be discounted. We are first and foremost to love God, and in our love for Him, others take a second seat.

And sometimes our obedience to Jesus Christ costs others. When we moved to France, it cost our children. It cost our extended families. It cost our friends, our church. Every fiber of me wanted to stay home. I didn't want to disappoint so many, particularly my children. But as we prayed through my distress, I realized God asked Patrick and me to do this, to obey no matter what it cost. While I certainly don't condone stories where missionaries follow what they think to be God's will at the expense of their children, I do understand the radical nature of the call of Christ. And in retrospect, stateside, I see that our move away actually was the best thing to happen to our family. Our trials there cemented our family, brought cohesiveness and camaraderie. However, before we left, we knew none of this.

Sometimes our obedience to Jesus Christ costs others.

In that state, I came across a quotation by Oswald Chambers that helped me move forward. He wrote, "If we obey God it is going to cost other people more than it costs us, and that is where the sting comes in. We can disobey God if we choose, and it will bring immediate relief to the situation, but shall be a grief to our Lord. Whereas if we obey God, He will look after those who have been pressed into the consequences of our obedience. We have simply to obey and leave all consequences with Him."[2] While I adored my children and loved my life in the States, I loved Jesus more. The thought of grieving Him propelled me to the Riviera.

CELEBRATE THE UNIQUE WAY GOD WORKS IN OTHERS

I am guilty of thinking that God works the same way He works in me as He does in you. But just as God is multifaceted and cannot be fully understood, so are the people He creates. He relates to us in us-shaped ways. To presume He must work a certain way circumvents His creativity. Oswald Chambers wrote, "Never make a principle out of your experience; let God be as original with other people as He is with you."[3]

When I sought to learn about the Holy Spirit in college, I attended some pretty wild meetings where folks chattered in tongues, fell over, and rolled around. They told me that if I wanted to be fully alive in Christ and experience His Spirit within me, I would of course speak in tongues, that a heavenly language would prove His existence inside me. To be honest, the spectacle scared me, so I retreated to my room and tried to sort it all out. I searched the Scriptures. I wrote letters to people I trusted. I asked advice. I wrestled. I endured folks trying to push me over with the force of their palm against my head. I stood firm, feet planted, determined that if God wanted to knock me out, He would. The surprise of it all came in the quietness of my dorm room, me kneeling on the linoleum floor, asking for more of Jesus in my life. Another language erupted from my lips, not in a huge show or under the watchful eyes of those who wanted to force the issue. No, this little gift came to me alone, in a perfect Mary-shaped way.

That story reminds me to trust the action of God in others' lives, not to judge them if they worship differently, speak to God differently, or attend a different denomination. We who love Jesus are all His, and He dynamically impacts us all. A lot of our angst with others centers on our preconceived design for their lives. We think we know what's best or what's right for them. And when they violate our perceived boundaries, we judge. Thinking that way can become a barrier.

A lot of our angst with others centers on our preconceived design for their lives. We think we know what's best or what's right for them. And when they violate our perceived boundaries, we judge. Thinking that way can become a barrier.

I remember a particular friend, how I wrestled to let her go into

God's sweet, beautiful hands. He has a plan for her life, a unique blueprint just for her. Her journey is not mine. In between us there have been misunderstanding and heartache. The kind of stuff only God can untangle. But He's big enough, isn't He? I choose today to let Him be original in her life, to do genesis things in her heart, to renew her steps in ways I can't even fathom.

That's one of the million reasons why I'm not God and He is. He perfectly understands every individual on this earth. He knows how to love, woo, change, transform, and bless each person. He knows how to discipline in just the right way.

He, as God of the universe, lets all of us exercise free choice. Why can't I let others, particularly my friend, exercise hers?

God has orchestrated unique things in my life. He has performed unique things in her life. As far as it depends on me, I must reconcile, but it takes two. So I let her go. And I let her rest in God's hands, knowing that He is the keeper of every single heart—even the hearts that break each other's and His. As I do this, I grow less dependent on others' opinions and more connected to God's.

There's freedom in that. We don't have to connive behind the scenes being someone's conscience or dictator. Letting God be God and us be us allows freedom not only for the person we're tempted to control but also for all of us who grow tired of such things.

CONFRONT TENDERLY

I've told the Lord many times that I don't want a ministry of confrontation. I'd rather sever an arm than have to talk to a friend about sin. Although I wouldn't say it's normative in my life, God has, on occasion, asked me to do something very hard—something that challenges my connection to others for my worth.

Not only does He ask us to examine our unhealthy connections, He tests our allegiance, our fidelity to the church. Why? Because the confrontation He asks us to do ultimately affects the unity of the church and its mission. When another believer blatantly sins and is left unchecked, the world notices. People get hurt. How many times have the unsavory actions of those who call themselves Christians tarnished the beauty of the church? How many people have been turned off by church because of the actions of others? Tragically some leave the church forever. I wonder how much of this could be salvaged by our simple obedience to confront our brothers and sisters in love.

The truth? Sometimes bullies in the church need to be confronted. Predators, left unchecked, will ruin people's lives. How do we stop these folks? By being kind? By ignoring them? No, God's avenue for health in His church is confrontation.

Sometimes bullies in the church need to be confronted.

None of us like it—and if we do, then we have other issues to deal with.

But Jesus makes our confrontation quite simple by starting small. If we've been sinned against, we go to the person directly. We don't gossip about it or ask a friend for advice. This is usually the hardest part of the process. Jesus said,

> If another believer sins against you, go privately and point out the offense. If the other person listens and confesses it, you have won that person back. But if you are unsuccessful, take one or two others with you and go back again, so that everything you say may be confirmed by two or three witnesses. If the person still refuses to listen, take your case to the church. Then if he or she won't accept the church's decision, treat that person as a pagan or a corrupt tax collector. (Matt. 18:15–17 NLT)

Not an easy passage! If God asks us to confront and it doesn't go well, others will need to get involved, which adds to the potential of heartache. Ultimately it becomes a decision of church leadership, where the result might be treating the person like an outsider (because isn't that how he or she is acting anyway?).

Confrontation feels icky because it's no longer a normative practice in our churches. We love harmony at any cost, and we fall too far on grace and not enough on God's holiness. In that, we cheapen grace. Dietrich Bonhoeffer, the twentieth-century pastor who defied Hitler, wrote, "Cheap grace is the preaching of forgiveness without requiring repentance, baptism without church discipline, Communion without confession, absolution without personal confession. Cheap grace is grace without discipleship, grace without the cross, grace without Jesus Christ."[4] Real grace forces sin out into the forefront, calls it the hellish thing it is, and counters it with redemption. Genuine grace means bringing sin to light, no longer shoving it in the back room of hushed conversations. Grace explodes in that sort of vulnerable, real light.

Even so, we deal with humans when we confront. It's important for us to employ the golden rule when we bring up sin to a friend. Confront the way you'd like to be confronted. Be kind, gentle. Be willing to be wrong in your perceptions. Affirm the person's worth and your relationship while you ask lots of questions to clarify. Paul summed it up well when he wrote, "Dear brothers and sisters, if another believer is overcome by some sin, you who are godly should gently and humbly help that person back onto the right path. And be careful not to fall into the same temptation yourself" (Gal. 6:1 NLT).

What does this have to do with growth? Everything. It's placing our hearts and reputations in the hands of God. It opens up the possibility for misunderstanding where we'll have to rely on His shoring up our reputation rather than our micromanaging it. When we confront, we must first examine ourselves, checking ourselves for logs before we pick splinters. This is part of renewing our minds, asking God to show us where we're thinking and acting wrongly. Confronting should be a humbling thing, a prospect that keeps us dependent on God. And as we walk through it, we'll soon find out whether we are confrontable or not. Because Everything Christians aren't people who simply enact Matthew 18; they are people who can receive confrontation with grace.

• • •

When people grow bigger than God in our lives, we can live in fear of others, never confronting. Or we can value someone's opinion so much, we lose our own. Ultimately when others have more power over us than God does, we shortchange our walk with Jesus. We fall into control or fear or despair. But no one has the ultimate power to separate us from God's love and His purposes for our lives. Our high view of Him should color our view of people. Even Jesus didn't entrust Himself fully to others: "Now when he was in Jerusalem at the Passover Feast, many believed in his name when they saw the signs that he was doing. But Jesus on his part did not entrust himself to them, because he knew all people and needed no one to bear witness about man, for he himself knew what was in man" (John 2:23–25).

We who are clay-footed also know what is in man. We simply have to look inside ourselves to see a heart's penchant for hiding and darkness and ill thoughts. Which makes it hard to love ourselves, let alone others. I'm thankful that God overcomes, that His grace enables us to offer grace to ourselves and grace to others. But more than that, I'm thankful that even if we walk this world with enemies around, He will sustain us, grow us, and keep us sure-footed.

QUESTIONS FOR REFLECTION AND DISCUSSION

- *Who is a giant in your life? How have that person's opinions of you mattered more than God's?*

- *How would it change your life right now if you chose to become dispassionate about certain people in your life?*

- *Think of someone who rubs you the wrong way. Why do you think the person does that? How has God uniquely created that person? How can you celebrate God's creativity in that friend?*

- *Has God pressed you to confront someone? Did you follow through? What lessons did you learn as a result? How did you grow in the aftermath?*

- *Why is it hard to let God convict someone else?*

chapter Five

Set Aside Worry

Don't worry about anything; instead, pray about everything.
Tell God what you need, and thank him for all he has done.

—Philippians 4:6 nlt

I woke up this morning with a song refraining through me. It wasn't the usual singsongy pop song that annoys; it was a choral arrangement I sang in high school, *"Dona Nobis Pacem."* The Latin words have a holy undertone. Turns out they mean, "Grant us peace," and they're part of the Catholic mass. Ironic that these words wormed their way into my mind on a morning when transition overwhelmed me. My husband began a new job ten days ago with a start-up company. It's already proving to be a great move, but not without its risks. My eldest, Sophie, starts college classes in ten days. And I'm sitting here on a Thursday in the middle of the fulcrum of so much change with "grant us peace" singing to me. Ten days ago our lives changed. Ten days from now they will change again. And His offer of peace permeates it all.

- I'd rather fret.
- I'd rather plot.

- I'd rather embrace fear as a friend.
- I'd rather not live in the mystery of transition.

But here I am, small and needy, facing a beautiful upheaval where our family morphs from five to four, and the sovereign God of everything whispers *Dona Nobis Pacem* over me as I wake.

Worry is a weighty monster with poisoned tentacles. It clutches at us, grabs at our minds, steals our breath, our will. It lurks. It pounces. It colors how we perceive the world. But God whispers peace in the midst. Me? I listen to my frenetic shouting, preferring my self-imposed rants, and I don't hear the Almighty's peace. These words of Oswald Chambers pin me to the ground: "The one great crime on the part of the disciple, according to Jesus Christ, is worry. Whenever we begin to calculate without God, we commit sin."[1] What would our lives look like if we refused to worry? How often are we guilty of the great crime of worry?

I worry about money. I worry about reputation. I worry about my children. I worry about my husband. I worry about worry. I worry about everything, actually. But it's sin. Plain and undecorated. We wrongly think we must be the salvation to our problems. And when we can't fix the problems (as is often the case), we fret. Romans 14:23 states it well: "Whatever does not proceed from faith is sin."

Worry involves both omission and commission. Omission because we forget God's faithfulness. Commission because we actively believe our abilities supersede His.

I met with Grace, a woman I'd met only online. She sat across from me in a hotel restaurant. From overseas, she had been on a quest across the United States with very little provision and even less fear. She rejoiced in the places she had seen. She told me of a family she met in another state who invited her to be a part of their family reunion. She recounted the story of attending a retreat for very little money, all provided by Jesus. She intimidated me by her ability to trust, and I say that in the nicest way. Her ability to leave behind worry stunned and beckoned me all at once. While we ate together, she shared her life, told me more of her story. Then she asked, "Have you read Habakkuk 3:17–19 in the Amplified Bible?"

"No," I said.

She smiled. "Well, you must then." She darted a look at the hotel's ceiling as if she would retrieve the memory there, then settled her eyes on mine and said, "Though the fig tree does not blossom and there is no fruit on the vines, [though] the product of the olive fails and the fields yield no food, though the flock is cut off from the fold and there are no cattle in the stalls, Yet I will rejoice in the Lord; I will exult in the [victorious] God of my salvation! The Lord God is my Strength, my personal bravery, and my invincible army; He makes my feet like hinds' feet and will make me to walk [not to stand still in terror, but to walk] and make [spiritual] progress upon my high places [of trouble, suffering, or responsibility]!"

The words that caught me were "my personal bravery." Could it be that God does what I cannot do? I'm so terrible at bravery. I'm much more adept at shrinking back. But God promises He'll be our bravery. Our worry results from finagling without God. Without Him, we're our personal bravery, which falls terribly short. With Him as our personal bravery, we calculate our lives alongside Him.

Worry and fear arrive when we forget that God is big, capable, and strong. We forget that He never forgets. Nothing escapes His notice. He is the most intelligent being in the universe, one billion times one billion Einsteins and then some. So why should I fret with Him at the helm?

Still, I do. I've coddled worry, as have you, I'm sure. Recently I received an angry e-mail from someone, demeaning me, questioning my calling. In that space of obvious negative feedback, I withdrew. I let one person's opinion taint how I viewed everyone else. I worried that others felt the same way about me, so I retreated, licked my e-mail wounds, and lived scared.

I cannot live that way, and neither can you. We cannot let the haters of this world define us. Or frighten us into no longer being ourselves. Which goes to show that no matter who we are or what we do, we must be ourselves, and in so doing, we'll make people angry. If we live safe lives, always afraid of what others think, we'll live in the land of vanilla.

We cannot let the haters of this world define us. Or frighten us into no longer being ourselves.

We shouldn't live our lives in reaction to a bully's comments.

One of my favorite movies, *Strictly Ballroom*, illustrates our bent toward worry. The dancing protagonist, Scott Hastings, gets in trouble for deviating from others' expectations, gaining enemies aplenty—even in his home. His father bowed to the dancing federation and capitulated to its prescribed dance routines. He danced the same old steps. But Scott gives up everything, even fame within the dancing community, to dance *his* way. In the last scene, his father says this: "We had the chance but we were scared. We walked away. We lived our lives in fear!"

You have the chance right now to be yourself. To love or work or perform or dance or sing or be uniquely you. Here's a warning. Some people won't like it. Some will send you letters about your errant ways. Some might ridicule you. Don't let that criticism shake you or make you shrink from being yourself. Be all you. Next time you're criticized, try to shake hands with it, not as a statement of your worth, but as a way to grow your faith—a way to stand against worry. And then boldly dance your steps.

Some of us don't know how to let go of our fears, our conundrums. The scripture at the beginning of this chapter is simple, yet instructive. To walk away from worrywart lives, we pray. We give something we value to God, letting its outcome rest there, too, without taking it back. That's how it is with our relationships too. There are many relationships I've placed in God's hands, willingly (sometimes) giving the outcome to Him. In some instances He surprised me with reconciliation; other times I learned patience in the waiting. But in all of that, He was (and is) sovereign.

- What do you hold tightly today? What causes undue worry?
- Is it something you created? A blog post, a piece of art, your job?
- Is it stress about finances or your future?
- Is it a broken-beyond-belief relationship?
- Is it fear about the next step God's asking you to take?

I can't guarantee you'll love the outcome if you pray the prayer below, but I can say that in praying it I've experienced peace, knowing the sovereign God of the universe, the One who flung the stars into existence, is big enough to carry the things we clutch to ourselves.

THE WORRYWART PRAYER

Dear Jesus, I give You _____. I humble myself before You, believing that You are bigger than I am, that You are more than capable to handle my burdens. I don't know what the outcome of my giving up control of _____ will be, but even so, I open my fist and let You grab it (or the person) from me. I want Your will. I want Your presence. I need Your strength. Please take this burden today, and use it in my life for Your glory. Help me to entrust _____ to You even when things seem dark. I trust You. At least I try. But help me to trust You today. Right now. I give it up. I choose not to worry anymore about this. Amen.

After you've prayed and let your worry rest on the sovereign One's shoulders, your next reaction is to be proactive. Worry's opposite is confidence. But what is confidence?

CONFIDENCE DOES NOT DEPEND ON CIRCUMSTANCES

We can be in the pits of emotional despair, up to our eyeballs in raging rivers of trials, or feel battle weary as war erupts around us—and yet be confident. Trials cannot steal our confidence unless we let them. Even raging rivers cannot shake our confidence: "If a river rages, he is not alarmed; he is confident, though the Jordan rushes to his mouth" (Job 40:23 NASB). Or when enemies seen or unseen threaten us, we can still be confident in God's ability to walk us through:

> *Though a host encamp against me,*
> *My heart will not fear;*
> *Though war arise against me,*
> *In spite of this I shall be confident.* (Ps. 27:3 NASB)

GOD IS OUR CONFIDENCE

God supplies confidence. Not only that, He *is* confidence. The God of the universe who made stars with a whisper of His breath, who holds oceans in His palm, who fashioned redwood trees—He is *for* us, on our side. Without Him, we are like this:

> *So are the paths of all who forget God;*
> *And the hope of the godless will perish,*
> *Whose confidence is fragile,*
> *And whose trust a spider's web.* (Job 8:13–14 NASB)

We read in Proverbs 3:26: "The LORD will be your confidence and will keep your foot from being caught" (NASB). Even when we're young, God promises to be our confidence: "You are my hope; O Lord GOD, You are my confidence from my youth" (Ps. 71:5 NASB). We don't have to conjure up confidence; He grants it: "Such confidence we have through Christ toward God. Not that we are adequate in ourselves to consider anything as coming from ourselves, but our adequacy is from God" (2 Cor. 3:4–5 NASB).

God Gives Confidence in Impossible Situations

In fact, God majors in impossibility: "Now, Lord, take note of their threats, and grant that Your bond-servants may speak Your word with all confidence" (Acts 4:29 NASB). Even when we are threatened, worried, helpless, or afraid, God will give us confidence to speak the truth in love. Because of Jesus' death on the cross, we can confidently approach God. For those who struggle with God's great acceptance, soak yourselves in this: "Let us draw near with confidence to the throne of grace, so that we may receive mercy and find grace to help in time of need" (Heb. 4:16 NASB; also see Eph. 3:12).

Our ability to boldly come to the Father is a gift, wrapped in the gift of Jesus' death and resurrection.

What a gift! We don't have to cower in fear beneath the titanic throne of God; we can approach Him as a child who knows his King as Father. We can scramble up the steps, onto the throne, into the lap of our heavenly Father because of what Jesus did on the cross. Our confidence is a result of His sacrifice for us. Our ability to boldly come to the Father is a gift, wrapped in the gift of Jesus' death and resurrection.

Confidence Is Something God Wants Us to Hold On To

We don't casually cultivate confidence; it's something we must grasp. "Christ was faithful as a Son over His house—whose house we are, if we hold fast our confidence and boast of our hope firm until the end" (Heb. 3:6 NASB). Because confidence is so important and needed, the author of Hebrews instructed us not to throw it away (Heb. 10:25). And if we don't, there is reward in our confidence. It is something to be prized and cherished. Because of Jesus, we have confidence.

Throwing it away and giving in to worry are like saying, "Jesus, Your sacrifice was not enough. I can't approach the Father. I just can't. I've done too many terrible things, and I'm not strong enough." Jesus is enough. He is our everything. But we are not enough. Don't throw away your confidence in what He has done. Yes, we fail. Yes, we hurt others. Yes, we make a royal mess of things. True. But Jesus made a way. Don't let your sin keep you from the joy of relationship with your heavenly Father.

CONFIDENCE AND CONDEMNATION CAN'T COEXIST

Remember the story of the prodigal son? The father waited on tiptoes at the end of a dusty road, longing for his son to return. He didn't wait with a hammer; he stood with outstretched arms. God the Father welcomes you today because of the outstretched arms of His Son on the cross. Hold on to that. Keep that confidence. "Beloved, if our heart does not condemn us, we have confidence before God" (1 John 3:21 NASB). A condemning heart steals our confidence. If that is you, lay your condemning heart before God as an offering. He is the only One capable of taking it. In its place, He will give you confidence—confidence that He loves you, accepts you, delights in you, and holds you.

CONFIDENCE IS NOT THE SAME AS
ASSERTIVENESS AND PUSHINESS

It's a quiet knowing that God is in control, that He sees us and hears us. That no matter what may befall us, God is on the throne, and we can approach Him anytime because of Jesus' death and resurrection. Confidence is not an elusive quality that a fickle god dispenses on a whim. It is a promise, not because of our merit, but because of His.

• • •

To live Jesus-honoring lives, we put on confidence like a cloak to stave off the chill of worry. Last night I worried when I received a late-night phone call from my daughter. She'd been walking through a difficult relationship and didn't know how to face it. The issue felt too big for her, too adult, yet she faced it with a confidence I admired. Still, after I spent time with her on the phone, I watched the walls of my bedroom as I longed to sleep. My head, filled with my daughter's predicament, kept me awake for hours. Eventually sleep captured me. The morning brought news of Sophie's pain, but she's managing it well. I cannot be there for her. And in that separation, I can either give in to worry or choose to let everything rest in Jesus' capable arms. Right now I'm handing everything over to Him. I'm singing *"Dona Nobis Pacem"* over me, over her, over our family.

Worry is needless. It doesn't enhance our lives, give us joy, or produce a longing for renewal. It simply looks at the existing stress lurking in our lives, enlarges it to monster proportions, then immobilizes us from growth. Whenever you're tempted to give in to its prowess, remember Jesus, how He walked this earth. He never rushed, didn't fluster. He certainly didn't let others' opinions of Him prevent Him from performing His mission. He lived peace, this Prince of Peace, by subjugating every potential stress under the sovereign authority of His Father. He rested there, as should we.

QUESTIONS FOR REFLECTION AND DISCUSSION

- *What worry currently seems like a monster to you?*

- *Recall a time in your life when you felt confident of God's hand in your life. Why did you have this confidence? Was it a choice on your part, or did the circumstances in your life make it easier to have peace?*

- *Look back over the Habakkuk passage in the Amplified Bible. What would it look like for God to be your personal bravery? What prevents you from believing He is?*

- *Who in your life is a worrywart? Why is he or she that way, in your opinion?*

- *Last year, what caused you the most worry? How would you handle the situation today in light of what you've read?*

Chapter Six

Practice Resilience

*Resilience is an ability to recover from or adjust
easily to misfortune or change.*

—*Merriam-Webster Dictionary*[1]

I WAKE THIS MORNING WITH AN URGENCY TO READ A PAS-
sage of Scripture that's grown mundane to me. It's almost cliché, so
much so that when I hear or read the words, I nearly roll my eyes. "I
know the plans I have for you, declares the LORD, plans for welfare and
not for evil, to give you a future and a hope." (Do I even need to cite it?
Jer. 29:11.) Why the eye rolling? Because this verse is ripped from its
context, stitched to pillows, repeated by well-meaning people to those
who grieve. I cannot bear it.

I heard that verse after my first pregnancy—an ectopic one—in
subtle rephrases.

- "God will use this pain. You'll be more empathetic."
- "It's not His will that you suffered."
- "Something amazing will come of this experience."
- "Just think of the story you'll tell."

Years later, the pain of losing my first child still pains me. Of course I understand that God has great plans for His people. I've seen that in my life, how He graciously and meticulously rescued me from my pain, myself, my sin-entrenched ways. But we've stripped these powerful words of their message. We've lost the context and therefore lost the significance.

In Jeremiah 28, we meet the prophet Hananiah. He prophesied in the midst of the nation of Israel's exile. They had been carted off to Babylon, juxtaposed into the fabric of a pagan nation, coming to the realization that the God who led them through the Red Sea sent them deliberately to an awful place. The then-defunct nation of Israel wanted relief. The people needed understanding. They craved clarity.

I've felt the weight of exile—in places where I wrestled with the nature of God's complete sovereignty over the universe (and subsequently my life) while awful circumstances choked me. During the ectopic pregnancy, I hollered these faithless words, "Now I have proof You don't love me!" I tear-stained my pillow as our marriage devolved into pain and misunderstanding. I shook my head when God relocated our family again, me the girl who wants only roots, not wings.

Exile.

In times like these, Hananiah is my dear friend. He used God-laced words: "Thus says the LORD of hosts, the God of Israel" (Jer. 28:2). (When I read these words, I place my name in Israel's place: "Thus says the LORD of hosts, the God of Mary.") He continued, "I have broken the yoke of the king of Babylon. Within two years I will bring back to this place all the vessels of the LORD's house, which Nebuchadnezzar king of Babylon took away from this place and carried to Babylon. I will also bring back to this place Jeconiah the son of Jehoiakim, king of Judah, and all the exiles from Judah who went to Babylon, declares the LORD, for I will break the yoke of the king of Babylon" (vv. 2–4). What a blessing! What a promise! The exiles will return to Jerusalem.

Hananiah uttered these words to Jeremiah in the house of the Lord.

It seems like a holy declaration, a longing amen. All will be well. Shalom will reign.

How many messages do we hear today that echo this prophet's words? Things will change; they have to. Surely God won't put you through more than you can bear, right? Another one of those verses yanked from context bothers me in this moment: "No temptation has overtaken you that is not common to man. God is faithful, and he will not let you be tempted beyond your ability, but with the temptation he will also provide the way of escape, that you may be able to endure it" (1 Cor. 10:13). This verse refers to temptations, not life's circumstances. God will provide a way to say no when you want to say yes to sin. But this verse doesn't promise that God will cease from putting you through more than you can bear.

Hananiah didn't remember that God often acts counterintuitively to our desired outcome. He disciplines the ones He loves.

Recently I recounted to God all the circumstances He's brought me through. When growth flourished, the scenery of my life looked like drought. Babylonian Nebuchadnezzer reigned in those moments, with exile as my yoke. He rained on my perceived joy-parade. In prayer, I asked God why, why, why all these hard places pressed me, sometimes to the point of breaking. He answered (aptly) with Scripture. "I discipline the ones I love," He told me (Heb. 12:6).

The truth: God puts us through more than we can bear.

He does.

Why?

Because after we journey through those places, we learn resilience. And that resilience brings the ability to joyfully live in the moment despite our circumstances—a holy paradox.

How many messages do we hear today that echo this prophet's words? Things will change; they have to. Surely God won't put you through more than you can bear, right?

God placed the nation of Israel in exile for a specified amount of time. He did it because of their rebellion, their world-bent ways. They lost sight of His heart to draw all nations to Himself, using Israel as His light. They neglected His commandments. They flirted, then played the harlot with pagan gods. Their distinctiveness from the cultures surrounding them dissolved to gray.

Are we any different?

> *Who are we to think that God should be in the business of relieving our pain, particularly when the pain has significant meaning to us? He presses us, disciplines us for a season, but we would rather circumvent the lesson and flirt with Babylon.*

Who are we to think that God should be in the business of relieving our pain, particularly when the pain has significant meaning to us? He presses us, disciplines us for a season, but we would rather circumvent the lesson and flirt with Babylon. We settle for sound-bite Christianity, believing the lie that God is more interested in our comfort than our hearts before Him.

Hananiah was prone to drama as he uttered his God-words. He broke a yoke of wood to illustrate his words. Yet listen to how God responded: "Thus says the LORD: You have broken wooden bars, but you have made in their place bars of iron. For thus says the LORD of hosts, the God of Israel: I have put upon the neck of all these nations an iron yoke to serve Nebuchadnezzar king of Babylon, and they shall serve him, for I have given to him even the beasts of the field" (Jer. 28:13–14). God's purposes for Israel at the time were to learn to survive and thrive under exile. God even willed that their economic stability be yoked to Babylon.

Jeremiah's last words to Hananiah were pointed: "Listen, Hananiah, the LORD has not sent you, and you have made this people trust in a lie" (28:15). He then predicted Hananiah's death, which came to pass that year.

We, too, have listened to the Hananiahs of our day. We want to believe the lie that the Christian life is all about our comfort and happiness; surely it's never about suffering or working hard or bearing up or being resilient. It can't be about God's disciplining us or growing us. We would rather grow in a flowered garden, not be exiled to the tumbleweed desert. Yet we can't escape the fact that God disciplines those He loves. He sometimes sends us to hard, pressing places.

We let our eyes skim over Paul's words about God bringing him more than he could bear: "We do not want you to be ignorant, brothers, of the affliction we experienced in Asia. For we were so utterly burdened beyond our strength that we despaired of life itself. Indeed, we felt that we had received the sentence of death. But that was to make us rely not on ourselves but on God who raises the dead. He delivered us from such a deadly peril, and he will deliver us. On him we have set our hope that he will deliver us again" (2 Cor. 1:8–10).

Jeremiah wrote a letter to the exiles in chapter 29. That's the context of the oft-repeated verses. He instructed them to marry and bury in exile, to plant vineyards and see their fruit become wine. He even encouraged the Israelites to seek the prosperity of their place of exile. And although Hananiah said only two years would pass before they were brought back to Jerusalem, Jeremiah reminded them that while it would be a long sojourn in exile, ultimately God would prosper them and give them hope.

This is a poignant picture of our lives here on earth. The New Testament is replete with exile imagery. We are aliens on this earth, a peculiar people. We are now the light on a hill, shining Jesus to the world. We are held tandem between the now and the not yet, what is today and what will be when the new heaven and the new earth dawn. Ultimately God will give us a glorious future. But today we must seek the prosperity of the people here, suffer well in exile from our true home, love others when we'd rather slander, bless the poor.

God's heart in Jeremiah's famous verse is not that we escape our lot, but that we learn to thrive in the midst of it. Jesus uttered this same truth: "I have told you all this so that you may have peace in me. Here on earth you will have many trials and sorrows. But take heart, because I have overcome the world" (John 16:33 NLT). He is our future, our hope. He is the place we go when this heavy world presses in. He enables us to grasp that elusive resilience. He doesn't remove us from pain. He uses the pain in our lives to discipline us, to make us ready to love Him more and bring more folks to His footstool.

God's heart in Jeremiah's famous verse is not that we escape our lot, but that we learn to thrive in the midst of it.

This world in which we rejoice, cry, worry, love, hope, and fear is a passing shadow. And we learn the art of resilience in the midst of it, with dirtied hands and worn-out feet. God doesn't remove; He brings us through. Exile burns a sustainable resilience into us. The kind of resilience where we learn to be faithful in little and do unnoticed things without complaint.

In thinking about resilience, a hallmark of living an Everything life, I unearth an old blog entry in France where I hunger for Jesus and He meets me:

Walking the children to school today, I searched for Jesus. He lives in France, too.

I saw Him in the eyes of a frizzy-haired, dog-walking woman whose eyes reek indifference. I saw Him at the little memorial of the village church's courtyard where cyclamen declared honor for war-killed vets. I felt Him as Julia held my hand, her pale white fingers engulfed in mine. I experienced Him when I apologized to Aidan and Julia for my grumpy mood this morning and they joyfully offered me grace and acceptance and friendship. I saw Him in the faces of so many French people, folks who I hope will someday be my friends.

Last night on my bed, I recounted my day. I was saddened by my parental neglect, how I didn't engage fully with my children and grumbled when they needed homework help. I remembered some of our most treasured times around a classic book and vowed to find some good books to read aloud to them, to once again make family reading a ritual.

I remembered our family rhythm and routine and how we've been ousted from it for several months now. I asked the Lord to please help us create a holy rhythm to our days, our weeks, our months. I realized that although my children have hiked to the top of a mountain, I haven't. (I was sick at the time.) I have yet to take a bike ride. I have yet to really stop and rest. I have yet to pursue things that deeply connect me to Jesus. I asked Jesus to please reconnect me—to Him, to my children, to my husband, to this life He has called me to in France.

And then I prayed that He and I would be close here. That I wouldn't be satisfied with just hurrying through a day, disturbed in spirit, devoid of Presence. "Dear Jesus, I love You," I told Him. "I want to be so close. So close. Hold me. Teach me that Your nearness is my good."

So, this morning I awoke with a twinge of anticipation, and that's when I saw Jesus everywhere. Today I read this from Oswald Chambers: "It is inbred in us that we have to do exceptional things for God; but we have not. We have to be exceptional in the ordinary things, to be holy in mean streets, among mean people, and this is not learned in five minutes."[2]

Like yours, my life is ordinary. I walk mean streets. I dream of big mountains of spiritual refining, but often get bogged down in the sheer ordinariness of life. Yet it's that daily grind of struggle, of gratitude in the midst of it, that brings me deeper, closer.

I walk the mean streets of France, gripping the hand of the One who is exceptional in my ordinary life.

. . .

We may live ordinary lives, but we are indwelt by an extraordinary God who can bring light from darkness, joy from despair. He desires that we develop resilience, such a simple, yet powerful trait, as we pursue an Everything life. One that I struggle with today.

Many of us need to get a grip, but we can't seem to find a handle to grab, and life sometimes pelts us. Growing like crazy seems ridiculously distant in this exile land. And resilience seems like a joke. Today I sent an e-mail of frustration to a few close friends, venting my worry, laying my heart bare. My day didn't magically improve. I didn't experience Jeremiah 29:11 prosperity. What did happen: my friends surrounded me, prayed for me, and loved me back to a semblance of joy. They were Jesus with skin on, crying alongside me. More than my current sadness, what I really needed was Jesus. He showed up. Whispered His love, and wooed me back. "He bowed the heavens and came down" (Ps. 18:9).

Because He is everything.

QUESTIONS FOR REFLECTION AND DISCUSSION

- *How has a typical reading of Jeremiah 29:11 brought you hope? How does knowing the verse in context change the way you think about your life today?*

- *Who are the Hananiahs of our day? Why is it easy to listen to them? Or is it?*

- *When have you been most resilient? Least? Why?*

- *How has your life felt like exile?*

- *Embracing your identity as an alien on this earth isn't easy. Why is that so? What in your life fights against that?*

Heart—Who We Are

JESUS TALKED A LOT ABOUT HEART IN THE GOSPELS. HE railed against religious leaders who seem cool on the outside but are angry, conniving, jealous, and full of judgment on the inside. He said what's inside us (our hearts) flows out of our mouths. Ultimately our actions reveal what's inside.

That's why it's impossible to live an abundant life by superimposing rules on ourselves. Without a changed heart, our lives become elaborate stage productions, easily dismantled after the show. Jesus is after reality, after truth. He is *the* truth.

To live authentic, invitational lives, our lives must flow like rivers from the inside out. When we meet Jesus and lay our will before Him, He invades our hearts, exchanges our nature for His, and sets our feet on a journey of living out and grasping for all the amazing things He's given us.

But if our hearts are far from Him, if we insulate ourselves from His touch, we will not grow. In the following chapters we'll examine what a changed, beautified heart looks like. We'll see how grabbing at our control weakens God's control of our lives. We'll learn the importance of letting go, being broken, and embracing true healing. And we'll learn to be kind to ourselves in the process.

Chapter Seven

Be an Am

Indeed, the "right time" is now. Today is the day of salvation.

—2 Corinthians 6:2 NLT

As I've prayed about this book, seeking God for answers, I've felt microscopic and needy. Whispers taunted me about my unworthiness, my penchant to wander. And yet, as I've prayed, God has been clear to me about one important thing: we grow in the Great Right Now. He changes our hearts in this moment. Sure, we can point to the past and discern victories there, but we must not remain tethered to yesteryear. Nor can we pine for how we will grow when everything aligns appropriately.

God is the Great I Am. If we are to be like Him, we must understand the significance of heart-change now. I've lived in the Great Yesterday most of my life, constantly looking back, so much so that my spiritual neck has whiplash. I've spent years trying to figure out why things happened the way they did and how I could possibly heal enough to survive. My issues grew like leviathan, untamable. Insecurity raged. Fear escalated. Instead of being broken in the best possible way, to let God rebuild me, at times I gave in to despair. Some of the people who injured me in the past grew larger than the Texas sky, greater in influence than even my thoughts. In that backward glance, who I was at the time of injury swallowed up the Great I Am.

I've lived in the Great Yesterday most of my life, constantly looking back, so much so that my spiritual neck has whiplash.

A rearview perspective minimizes God. If you spend your life dwelling on those perceived giants, you prevent growth today because you're linked to the past with an iron chain. But you don't have to be victimized by your heart.

When I wrote *Building the Christian Family You Never Had*, I worried as I looked back. Petrified to write the first two chapters about my upbringing, I had to use every ounce of my courage (and it felt like a thimbleful) to simply find words, static and stark on a white piece of paper.

- Childhood rape
- Drug abuse in the home
- Divorces
- Death of a parent
- Neglect

I could barely write the words because I could feel the disapproving looks of my family as I did so. Every word felt like a victory in light of this. But even when I finished, I made sure the chapters went through vigorous edits. I gave permission to the editors to censure me if I stepped out of line or if my words sounded too harsh.

Eventually I had to share the chapters with my mom.

I didn't want to.

At the time I lived in France, where everything shifted beneath me, quaking my foundations. I wasn't in the best emotional space to experience her rejection. Or to have her tell me what I wrote was lies. I fretted that she'd withhold her love from me. In a very real way, my fear about her and about telling the truth about the past noosed me. It kept me choked, terrified.

When I sent the e-mail with the book attached, my stomach roiled. I lived in the land of dread, still hoping that all my fears about rejection and being called a liar would prove unfounded fancies, sparked from my overactive imagination.

My mom's words came back. And they were exactly what I feared.

- I was a liar.
- I wasn't worthy of love.
- How dare I share such things?

Counterintuitively the Mary who lived caged in the past broke free as something cracked inside. My mom, who had become as big to me as a Macy's parade character, exhaled to a spent party balloon. Tears streaking my face, I realized that what I feared most had materialized, yet I survived.

In that moment, I became Job, proclaiming, "What I always feared has happened to me. What I dreaded has come true" (Job 3:25 NLT).

I mirrored Dorothy, watching Toto pull back the curtain on the fear-inspiring wizard, only to see a small person on a stepstool.

I mirrored Dorothy, watching Toto pull back the curtain on the fear-inspiring wizard, only to see a small person on a stepstool.

And as I reflect on that crazy, courageous act right now, I picture the Lord in heaven with a smile across His face, thinking, *She is going to grow so much. I have such good plans for her, but she must first come to the place where she values My opinion of her over any other person's on this earth.*

I lived more afraid of my mom's opinion of me than of God's

surprising and generous approval. I stayed in the past, wallowing there, feeling unloved and forsaken. But the Great I Am beckons me today to be filled, to be loved, to be whole right now.

Bob George elaborates on the now-ness of growth: "The process of spiritual maturity is simply our learning to turn more and more areas of our lives over to Christ through faith. The past is over; the future isn't here yet. Therefore, living by faith can only be done in the present."[1] One of my favorite scriptures in the Old Testament testifies to this phenomenon as well. Take a moment to read the following verses from Isaiah 43:16–21:

> This is what the LORD says—
> he who made a way through the sea,
> a path through the mighty waters,
> who drew out the chariots and horses,
> the army and reinforcements together,
> and they lay there, never to rise again,
> extinguished, snuffed out like a wick:
> "Forget the former things;
> do not dwell on the past.
> See, I am doing a new thing!
> Now it springs up; do you not perceive it?
> I am making a way in the wilderness
> and streams in the wasteland.
> The wild animals honor me,
> the jackals and the owls,
> because I provide water in the wilderness
> and streams in the wasteland,
> to give drink to my people, my chosen,
> the people I formed for myself
> that they may proclaim my praise." (UPDATED NIV)

What surprises me about these verses is the magnitude of God's actions on behalf of the Israelites in the past. He performed great, amazing feats, drying up the Red Sea, drowning Israel's enemies, rescuing the Israelites from certain doom. And yet in verse 18, God clearly told them to forget all that. This perplexes me a bit because God chastised the Israelites many times for forgetting what He did. They wandered the wilderness because of their stubborn forgetfulness. But God's intention here is this: He wants His people to be receptive in the moment in order to be forward thinking. He wants us to have faith in His ability to do new things now. He is not interested in our dwelling on the past in a nostalgic way, where we become stuck in a particular place. He wants us to always advance, always move forward.

A friend of mine lost her husband. He wasn't a perfect man by any stretch, but after many years of living without him, she remembered him as a saint. Her entire life mourned the memory of him, and she could not move forward. She felt happiness only back then, when her husband held her hand, her heart. Beyond his death, nothing good emerged. She lived in the land of nostalgia. And living there, she stagnated and slipped into depression.

He wants us to heal so fully from the past that folks wouldn't know we even walked all those trails of tears.

For me, the publishing business is my nostalgia. I look back on past successes and want to stay there. But those close to me, my champions, keep me moving forward. There is always another risk God asks us to take. Always another adventure around the corner. But if we stay in the "good old days," we won't take those risks or live that adventure today.

A noble goal of living the Everything life is this forward heart momentum. God wants to do something new. He wants to create rivers where water languished, flowers where desert winds blew away all the foliage of our lives. He wants us to heal so fully from the past that folks wouldn't know we even walked all those trails of tears.

As I examine what the Lord has wrought in my heart, I know He has uncaged me. This is something I couldn't do on my own; it's His sheer gift of grace. I'm not a Pollyanna now, rejoicing when bad things happen. It's that my perspective on life is shifting from introspective pessimism to unhindered optimism.

I no longer need to be defined by the trials in the past. I am not Mary who suffered (though it is part of my story). I am Mary who has been set free. Because of Jesus' radical, freeing act on the cross and His mind-boggling resurrection, I don't need to wallow back there; I can rejoice here, now.

Yet we crawl back there, don't we? We camp in the "I was" statements rather than the "I am" statements.

- I was molested.
- I was abandoned.
- I was injured.
- I was a failure.
- I was sick.
- I was insignificant.
- I was overlooked.
- I was disobedient.
- I was wild.

God calls each of us to be an "am." Still, we live caged by our past, by our "I was" statements. These steel cages have become comfortable to us because they are known. The "I was" statements define us. We've made our nest in the past, letting shackled living become our normal. Soaring is too scary, too new. We'd rather live chained to our strange comfort zone.

Yet God, the Great I Am, wants to free us today. He longs for us to embody these verses:

We have escaped like a bird
  out of the fowler's snare;
the snare has been broken,
  and we have escaped.
Our help is in the name of the LORD,
  the Maker of heaven and earth. (Ps. 124:7–8 NIV)

A fowler is someone who snags a bird in a trap, a hunter who observes the behavior of birds to predict what they'll do next. Then he captures the bird based on its typical behavior. In like manner, Satan is our fowler. He knows our cages. He convinces us that the door to the cage is locked, that we can't flee. The truth? The door is open right now, but we're too afraid to fly.

Charles Spurgeon, in his commentary on fowlers, wrote this freeing sentence: "No bird of paradise shall die in the fowler's net."[2] We are, in this moment, birds meant to soar. My heart for you is that you'll experience uncaged, joyful freedom. That you'll be wily enough to silence the Enemy's lies that yell, "Your cage is locked! You're doomed to be stuck in the past!" That you'll take one step out of the door, away from the comfortable cage, and flex your wings a little. Dare to be brave today, and trust that when you extend your wings, you will fly.

It's time to make some "am" statements, to let go of the shackles of the past so we can anticipate the growth that God will bring right now.

- I was molested. *I am used by God to help others heal from molestation.*
- I was abandoned. *I am wanted and needed in God's kingdom.*
- I was injured. *I am healed by Christ's great sacrifice.*
- I was a failure. *I am renewed so I can try again.*
- I was sick. *I am well, thanks to God's presence in my sickness.*
- I was insignificant. *I am significant to Jesus.*
- I was overlooked. *I am noticed by the God who sees.*

- I was disobedient. *I am freely obeying the God who set me free.*
- I was wild. *I am wildly in love with Jesus.*

Whether our past was amazing or tragic, God calls us onward and upward, beckoning us away from past tense to present tense. Our future growth depends on our ability to be an "am." To live now, uncaged, unfettered, free. To live any other way borders on disobedience. The apostle Paul called living like we used to *slavery*. In this passage he was referring to living under the Law, but I believe when we tether ourselves to our pasts and stay stuck back there, we create our own legalism. He wrote, "For freedom Christ has set us free; stand firm therefore, and do not submit again to a yoke of slavery" (Gal. 5:1).

> Whether our past was amazing or tragic, God calls us onward and upward, beckoning us away from past tense to present tense.

I'd like you to spend some time with a pen and paper, asking yourself these four questions:

1. What would it look like for me to be an "am" today?
2. What "I was" statements have I made that prevent my growth?
3. What "I am" statements are true about me today?
4. What words have I believed about myself that keep me caged to my past?

Take a moment to pray after you've answered these questions, asking God to show you where you're living in the past. Trust that He is big enough to open your eyes to the things that prevent growth in your life. Be willing to let go of some of the statements that used to define you. Anticipate the dry places of your life that God wants to water. He does want to do a new thing today.

• • •

God desires your heart to live in freedom. He's certainly desired that mine did. He's taken a broken, needy girl who told the story of her upbringing just to get attention, and He's healed me from that story. As the Author and Perfecter of our faith, He writes a new story for each of us, a present-day reality. The question is, will you let Him write it in the everlasting today? And how will it be written? Past tense with little growth, or present tense with exponential growth?

As the Author and Perfecter of our faith, He writes a new story for each of us, a present-day reality.

I'll end with a little poem I wrote that challenges us to live now in light of the future we'd like to have:

Feel now how you'd like to feel someday.
Play now like you'd like to play someday.
Live now as you'd like to live someday.
Risk now how you'd like to risk someday.
Pray now like you'd like to pray someday.
Give now as you'd like to give someday.
Forgive now how you'd like to forgive someday.
Rest now like you'd like to rest someday.
Be now as you'd like to be someday.

QUESTIONS FOR REFLECTION AND DISCUSSION

- *What do you gain by being connected to the past?*

- *What is your comfort zone? What types of changes frighten you? Why?*

- *How have you viewed the past with nostalgia?*

- *If you could paint a picture of you living uncaged and free, how would your life look differently than it does today?*

- *Who is the freest person you know? How is that person's heart free? How do the person's actions define that freedom?*

Chapter Eight

Forsake the Seven-Letter Word That Demolishes Everything

Blessed are the meek, for they shall inherit the earth.
—Matthew 5:5

To celebrate the end of summer and to give our eldest daughter, Sophie, a last hurrah before she left for college, we rented Jet Skis. At first this seemed like a wise idea, particularly when I squeezed the accelerator and the lake whizzed by. But as we ventured into the belly of Lake Ray Hubbard and my son Aidan asked if he could take over, I rethought this outing. I jumped into the water and let Aidan take the helm, while Sophie and my youngest, Julia, determined to race us on the other Jet Ski. I balanced on the back of the idling machine as Aidan took control of the vehicle. When he felt the power in his right hand where he grabbed the throttle, he smiled. I knew I would die.

Instead I laughed. Laughed so hard my eyes watered as the lake and palatial homes blurred by.

We switched riders halfway through so Julia could ride with me. She is thirteen and adventurous and wholly inexperienced. But when she grabbed the helm, I didn't feel afraid. How could a small slip of a girl be dangerous? Oh, but she was. She jerked the Jet Ski heavenward, then killed the gas as we bucked in dangerous stops and starts down the lake's sidelines, narrowly avoiding protruding tree limbs and other motorcraft. When she turned, she fully decelerated, but when the craft straightened, she gunned it. I nearly flew off and died.

Instead I laughed.

In the recollection, I remember the line from an ancient song, "I'm about to lose control, and I think I like it."

CONTROL HURTS OUR GROWTH

If you haven't guessed it yet, *control* is the seven-letter word that demolishes everything. It's that thing we crave, grab at, sacrifice much of our hearts to have. We want to regulate the throttle of our lives and, if we're being honest, throttle the lives around us. It's okay if we alone navigate the Jet Ski, but let another cut in and we panic. Control is the inner disease of those who need stability and order to function. It is the shiny little idol we worship without noticing. When my life careened out of control as a child, when drug abuse tainted the parties my parents threw, when neighborhood boys stole my virginity, when I felt more like a burden than a blessing in my home, control hugged me. And it followed like a specter into my Christianity and adulthood.

> *Control is the inner disease of those who need stability and order to function.*

Control satiates me. It calms me. Nursing it helps me make sense of my world. When trials inevitably knock on my door, my response is to clean my house, align the cans in my pantry, create order from chaos. When God asks me to risk for His sake, I create lists in my head about why it's not logical to do so. I'd rather live a controlled life than let Jesus take me on unfamiliar roads.

Control is an untamed beast, particularly when we leverage it to manage our own public relations firm. Why? Because it's impossible to control how other people view us. And if we further extend our control to manipulate others, we'll slip into an impossible task because people don't relish being formed into our mold.

Control Blinds Us

Control can even blind us. We reason, oddly, that God is fine with us because we appear to be in control and everything on the outside of our lives is in order. Control keeps us distant from our hearts, our pet sins, and those things we hide. We forget how big God's reach is, that He can see right past our spiritual facades into our hearts.

King David addressed this issue after his fall with Bathsheba, the murder of her husband, and the subsequent cover-up. He attempted to control the circumstances in his life and cover up his sin. God sent Nathan the prophet to nail him with an all-too-true story. David repented, broken before God. Prior to that, he appeared kingly, righteous, in control. Yet he didn't fool God. In his anguish, David cried,

> *Going through the motions doesn't please you,*
> *a flawless performance is nothing to you.*
> *I learned God-worship*
> *when my pride was shattered.*
> *Heart-shattered lives ready for love*
> *don't for a moment escape God's notice.* (Ps. 51:16–17 MSG)

Could it be that we are guilty of flawless Christian performances? That we've taken up ownership and control of our relationship with Jesus? If we desire to live sustainable, growing lives, we must get to the place where we understand that our effort, even what we perceive to be holy effort, cannot accomplish God's purposes. Our need for control

*Could it be that
we are guilty of
flawless Christian
performances?*

shoves away God's ownership in our lives, and it keeps us at the helm. In relinquishing control, growth flourishes. We learn to trust the sovereign One with our lives, to no longer micromanage even our relationship with Him. That type of journey thrives from the inside out.

CURB CONTROL WITH AN EXCHANGED LIFE

We need an exchanged life where Christ woos and changes us. Bob George puts it simply,

> Jesus Christ identified with us in our death in order that we might be identified with Him in His resurrection. We give Christ all that we were—spiritually dead, guilty sinners—and Christ gives us all that He is—resurrected life, forgiveness, righteousness, acceptance. . . . Christians are continually trying to change their lives; but God calls us to experience the exchanged life. Christianity is not a self-improvement program. It isn't a reformation project. It is resurrection! It is new life! And it is expressed in terms of a total exchange of identity.[1]

We read these words and nod in assent. Of course we believe this, but we don't live it out. We naturally resort to controlling our Christianity instead of letting Jesus live His life through us.

We're into improvement plans, but we forget that God holds control over our lives. After all, "the heart of man plans his way, but the LORD establishes his steps" (Prov. 16:9). Even when we think we've got everything under control, with our expectations and plans aplenty, God still establishes our steps. He often will thwart our plans, pull the rug out from underneath our hopes, all for the sake of bringing us back to Him. God is like the wise man: "A wise man scales the city of the mighty and brings down the stronghold in which they trust" (Prov. 21:22). Because He loves us so much, He scales the walls of our hearts, exposing and pulling down that in which we trust. It's a painfully loving act.

Have you been in those places before? I felt that holy demolition overseas, where everything I trusted and relied on for happiness came tumbling down. My way of communicating? Taken. Money? Shaken. Relationships? Forsaken. In that place of true despair, I cried out with a shred of hope, only to find more taken from me. Like David, I had my pride shattered before me. My control dismantled. In that breaking down, God could finally get a word in heartwise. He scaled the city of my life, then asked me this question: "Am I everything?"

He hadn't been my everything, I hated to admit. Everything meant that my life played itself out according to my expectations. A stable life, a good income, a happy family, great kids, no relational discord, success in ministry. My everything meant my personal nirvana. So when God stripped everything away from me, I panicked. Like casualties of war, my dreams lay waste at my feet. And still God whispered, "Am I everything?"

He whispers that to you too. As He carefully dismantles the idol of control, He pushes the question. Is He everything?

When we control our hearts, we live manageable (at least on the surface) lives. We imagine ourselves safe, melting into the conglomeration of every other person who worships at the feet of control. When Jesus isn't our *everything*, our enough, we pursue every other thing that fills. Just like the rest of the world. But Jesus says we're not to live like everyone else. Our lives should be different, marked by fearlessness and bold belief. Consider His words: "Don't worry about these things, saying, 'What will we eat? What will we drink? What will we wear?' *These things dominate the thoughts of unbelievers*, but your heavenly Father already knows all your needs. Seek the Kingdom of God above all else, and live righteously, and he will give you everything you need" (Matt. 6:31–33 NLT, emphasis mine).

At the altar of control, we let many things dominate our thoughts. What frightens me about this passage is that the constant managing and worry are hallmarks of someone who doesn't believe in Jesus! Is that kind of earthly preoccupation Christianity? I worry that I'll live a bland life, where the Holy Spirit's dynamic power is easily explained away or flat out unseen. That folks would view me, my actions, my power, and never see God's energy behind it all.

CURE CONTROL WITH ABANDON

If the seven-letter word that demolishes everything is *control,* the seven-letter remedy is *abandon,* which on the surface seems like a pretty awful word. No one likes to be abandoned. Yet God asks us to abandon our control, to abandon all for the sake of Him. Why? Not to mess with us or make us miserable. Not to demolish our strongholds only to leave us barren. No, He asks us to abandon our control so that He can reign in our lives and grow us.

He asks us to abandon our control so that He can reign in our lives and grow us.

After death comes resurrection. Life. Growth. These derive only from God. Jesus endured the cross for the joy set before Him. Restoration blooms after deconstruction. The problem is we're too busy building our flimsy playhouses to realize that our building materials won't withstand even the calmest storms. Only God, the Master Carpenter, can tear us down to our foundations, show them to be shaky, create a new foundation on His rock, and build a new, stronger, resilient life—a mansion to His glory, His capability, not ours. Matthew 7:25 sums this up perfectly: "Though the rain comes in torrents and the floodwaters rise and the winds beat against that house, it won't collapse because it is built on bedrock" (NLT).

Lay it down. In this moment, as your eyes scan the words of this book, make a choice to abandon. To let go of your need to control your life, others' lives, and your heart. Rid yourself of this idol. Return to Jesus. Only He can remake you. Only He is in the business of resurrection.

• • •

As you take to your knees, read the words of Hosea 14. Ponder them. Ask God to show you where you've worshipped the god of your hands. Let Him reveal where He is not enough. Be willing to hear where you have trusted in other things. Repent. You who long for crazy growth will see it not because of your unction, but because of His action. He plants seeds, waters, and makes us grow like trees.

A Plea to Return to the LORD

Return, O Israel, to the LORD your God,
>> *for you have stumbled because of your iniquity.*
Take with you words
>> *and return to the LORD;*
say to him,
>> *"Take away all iniquity;*
accept what is good,
>> *and we will pay with bulls*
>> *the vows of our lips.*
Assyria shall not save us;
>> *we will not ride on horses;*
and we will say no more, 'Our God,'
>> *to the work of our hands.*
In you the orphan finds mercy."

I will heal their apostasy;
>> *I will love them freely,*
>> *for my anger has turned from them.*

I will be like the dew to Israel;
he shall blossom like the lily;
he shall take root like the trees of Lebanon;
his shoots shall spread out;
his beauty shall be like the olive,
and his fragrance like Lebanon.
They shall return and dwell beneath my shadow;
they shall flourish like the grain;
they shall blossom like the vine;
their fame shall be like the wine of Lebanon.

O Ephraim, what have I to do with idols?
It is I who answer and look after you.
I am like an evergreen cypress;
from me comes your fruit.

Whoever is wise, let him understand these things;
whoever is discerning, let him know them;
for the ways of the LORD are right,
and the upright walk in them,
but transgressors stumble in them. (Hos. 14)

According to Hosea, the remedy for a controlled life is repentance, turning away from our ways to God's ways. It's giving the throttle to Jesus, letting Him propel us forward instead of our navigating the Jet Ski. It's letting go, something so few of us relish. But as we learn the art of letting go of control, we'll begin to understand the abundance that Jesus promised His followers. To abandon all is to take our hearts, place them before the One who created them, and dare to believe He can live life powerfully through our surrendered lives.

QUESTIONS FOR REFLECTION AND DISCUSSION

- *When was the last time you felt out of control? Did you like it? Hate it? Why?*

- *What prevents you from abandoning your plans right now?*

- *What do you gain by being in control?*

- *Looking back over your life, what has been the single biggest contribution to your tendency toward control? Did you have a chaotic childhood? Did someone abandon you? Did circumstances spin out of control?*

- *What part of the Hosea passage spoke to you today? Why?*

EMBRACE HOLY INEBRIATION

Don't be drunk with wine, because that will ruin your
life. Instead, be filled with the Holy Spirit.

—EPHESIANS 5:18 NLT

I WATCHED THE EFFECTS OF ALCOHOL—AND OTHER MIND-altering substances—when I was far too young. At hazy joint parties, adults offered the little white "cigarette" to five-year-old me. I watched those people inhale, smile, and then act crazy. I watched as others gulped liquor and beer until they were cross-eyed drunk, falling all over me, themselves, and our spartan hippie furniture. In a random moment when one relative dared to tell me she loved me, her words slurred with alcohol breath. I watched other relatives stumble, eyes glassy. They needed the stuff so much that they couldn't face a day without it. I sat in a car attempting to pray as we veered left and right, lurching through the night, a drunk person at the helm. I spent hours alone while the adults in my life abandoned me to drink and drug. In the unholy sanctuary of that place, I decided that alcohol and any other mood-altering substance were pure evil.

In preparation for studying Luke 1 in church, my mind caught on a sentence, and I couldn't deviate from it. Tucked inside the angel Gabriel's heady words that Zechariah would be a father, his wife a mother, were these words about their upcoming son, John: "He will be great before the Lord. And he must not drink wine or strong drink, and he will be filled with the Holy Spirit, even from his mother's womb" (Luke 1:15). Given my background, this all made sense to me. Being holy meant abstaining from drink.

Gabriel's prohibition reminded me of a holy vow, called the Nazirite vow, in which those wishing to dedicate themselves fully to God must not touch drink: "The LORD spoke to Moses, saying, 'Speak to the people of Israel and say to them, When either a man or a woman makes a special vow, the vow of a Nazirite, to separate himself to the LORD, he shall separate himself from wine and strong drink. He shall drink no vinegar made from wine or strong drink and shall not drink any juice of grapes or eat grapes, fresh or dried. All the days of his separation he shall eat nothing that is produced by the grapevine, not even the seeds or the skins'" (Num. 6:1–4). In light of this, it seemed John would become a great, set-apart man for God, filled mightily with the Holy Spirit.

In several scriptures we find overdrinking and the Holy Spirit mentioned close together. On the day of Pentecost, at nine o'clock in the morning, bystanders accused the disciples of drunkenness when, really, they were filled up with the Holy Spirit: "All were amazed and perplexed, saying to one another, 'What does this mean?' But others mocking said, 'They are filled with new wine'" (Acts 2:12–13). Paul advised us not to resort to drunkenness, but to be filled with the Spirit instead: "Don't be drunk with wine, because that will ruin your life. Instead, be filled with the Holy Spirit" (Eph. 5:18 NLT).

In the Old Testament, we see a devout Hannah praying with such raw emotion and anguish that the priest accused her of drunkenness:

As she continued praying before the LORD, Eli observed her mouth. Hannah was speaking in her heart; only her lips moved, and her voice was not heard. Therefore Eli took her to be a drunken woman. And Eli said to her, "How long will you go on being drunk? Put your wine away from you."

But Hannah answered, "No, my lord, I am a woman troubled in spirit. I have drunk neither wine nor strong drink, but I have been pouring out my soul before the LORD. Do not regard your servant as a worthless woman, for all along I have been speaking out of my great anxiety and vexation."

Then Eli answered, "Go in peace, and the God of Israel grant your petition that you have made to him." (1 Sam. 1:12–17)

Eli mistook her devotion for drunkenness.

The Pharisees accused Jesus of being drunk: "The Son of Man came eating and drinking, and they say, 'Look at him! A glutton and a drunkard, a friend of tax collectors and sinners!' Yet wisdom is justified by her deeds" (Matt. 11:19).

Why dwell on the connection between intoxication and the Holy Spirit? As I consider John the Baptist, I see the wisdom of God in asking him to refrain from drink. Think about his quirkiness, his clothing, his diet. Remember his boldness and fearlessness. His behavior bent more toward outspoken oddball than straitlaced John Doe. This abstention, in addition to marking John as fully set apart for a particular Jesus-preparing task, shows us along with John's contemporaries that nothing influenced his antiestablishment behavior other than the Spirit within him. John's holy inebriation made him a standout. It's why others equated him with Elijah.

To correlate intoxication with the Holy Spirit feels blasphemous. Aside from the verses above, the Bible clearly states that getting drunk is bad. If we obsess over inebriation, we'll do stupid things and lead lazy, lackadaisical lives. (Read Proverbs to gain more insight.) And yet, truth tugs at me. What about intoxication seems to coincide with a Spirit-enlivened life? Should we who long to be more like

Jesus exist in a state of holy inebriation? Of course I'm not referring to some of the extra-bibilical accounts of late where people claim to be drunk in the Spirit. I'm not condoning foolishness or madness. But I do believe we can glean a few things about growth if we make the connection.

Here are eight ways the state of drunkenness applies to followers' Spirit-led lives:

1. THEY LACK INHIBITION

Our image-driven culture fosters inhibition. We're afraid to be "out there" like John the Baptist. And yet, if we walk by the Spirit, we've taken in a foreign substance (the Holy Spirit) who will inevitably control our actions. We aren't our own. The apostle Paul reiterated this truth that we've got the Spirit of the living God dwelling beneath our skin: "Don't you realize that your body is the temple of the Holy Spirit, who lives in you and was given to you by God? You do not belong to yourself, for God bought you with a high price. So you must honor God with your body" (1 Cor. 6:19–20 NLT).

Inhibition breeds reticence, makes us self-conscious, unable to behave in a relaxed and authentic way. It's acting contrary to what we think we should do. To lack inhibition means to do the opposite—to be real, true to ourselves. It's acting in conjunction with our belief systems. As followers of Jesus, a lack of inhibition should be our hallmark.

2. THEY DON'T CARE WHAT OTHERS THINK

When I flirted with drink in junior high and a bit into high school, I remember feeling this strange out-of-body sensation as I floated above myself, like some sort of apparition. I watched myself do things I wouldn't normally do. Stupid things. Embarrassing things. Things I would regret.

I didn't care what my friends thought, what those boys hanging out with us thought. I didn't even care what I thought. Deliciously emancipated from the expectations of others, I simply acted.

Although it's not wise to be impulsive (again, I fall back on the blessed book of Proverbs for guidance here), Spirit-inhabited believers should be so trusting of the Spirit's guidance that if He asks them to do something wacky or scary, they should follow, not worrying about what others feel in the moment. God asked me to strike up a conversation with a stranger in church, then stop and pray in the moment. He asked me to walk dusty Ghanaian roads through tenements to share Him with Muslim women sewing batik dresses on foot-pumped sewing machines. He told me to leave everything familiar, make our extended families furious, and bumble my way through southern France and church planting. What has He asked of you? Have you stopped before obeying, considering more what others think of you?

3. They Can't Get Enough of What Made Them Drunk

One drink isn't enough. And once we've had one, if we're an addictive type, we need more. Then more. Then more. If we become addicted to and controlled by drink (or other things), it takes more to fill us. Those addicted crave the next drink. Eventually they cannot live without a certain amount of alcohol in their systems.

The beauty of living by the Spirit is that Jesus promises us living water, the kind of drink that fully, truly satisfies us. In John 4, Jesus hung out with a desperate woman who had many husbands and then lived with a man. That day all she wanted was water, but what she really needed was Jesus. When He told her He could give her living water, her eyes lit up. I wonder if she thought Jesus peddled a magic elixir, a vial from the fountain of youth. Yet consider Jesus' response: "Everyone who drinks this water will get thirsty again and again.

The beauty of the Spirit-controlled life is that we have that artesian well within us. We can find satisfaction in Jesus. We can quench our thirst. We can addict ourselves to Jesus and not be disappointed or ashamed.

Anyone who drinks the water I give will never thirst—not ever. The water I give will be an artesian spring within, gushing fountains of endless life" (vv. 13–14 MSG). Human beings spend their lives searching for what fills them. This woman did. She looked for love and fulfillment in every possible way, yet Living Water personified stood before her, and He promised to slake her soul thirst.

The beauty of the Spirit-controlled life is that we have that artesian well within us. We can find satisfaction in Jesus. We can quench our thirst. We can addict ourselves to Jesus and not be disappointed or ashamed. Instead, we will be filled—and then some. And that overflowing will spill over into others' lives.

4. THEY CONSIDER EVERYONE A FRIEND

Being inebriated, controlled by another substance, helps people break down walls in their minds. Happy drunks say things like, "I love you, man." (Of course the opposite is sometimes true as well. Drunk folks get into rip-roaring fights.) I love how Jesus embodied a gathering-of-friends mentality. We see Him hanging out with all sorts of people, in every socioeconomic strata. He dined with folks from the Roman IRS, hung out with women of the night, and shared a table with outcasts. For those wanting friendship, He opened His arms wide, wide, wide.

Those of us who follow Jesus, who want to live lives like Him, must do the same, being careful not to show favoritism. James 2:1–4 is clear on this welcoming aspect of Holy Spirit living:

My dear brothers and sisters, how can you claim to have faith in our glorious Lord Jesus Christ if you favor some people over others? For example, suppose someone comes into your meeting dressed in fancy clothes and expensive jewelry, and another comes in who is poor and dressed in dirty clothes. If you give special attention and a good seat to the rich person, but you say to the poor one, "You can stand over there, or else sit on the floor"—well, doesn't this discrimination show that your judgments are guided by evil motives? (NLT)

We must allow the Holy Spirit within us to break down our perceived barriers of others so we can consider many different people as friends. This is not an easy process, nor is it intuitive. It starts with a willingness on our part to admit that the way we view people is flawed. We come to others with prejudices aplenty, judging before we have the chance to know someone. It's an act of our will to choose to see people simply as wildly loved by God, to assume their beauty before guessing their depravity.

5. THEY DON'T FILTER THEIR TRUE FEELINGS, THOUGHTS, AND EMOTIONS

I mentioned that I had a family member who told me she loved me when she was smashed. In the moment it made me hopping mad, but on another level, I felt relief that somewhere buried inside my stoic relative lived a heart that loved. Drunk people typically don't have walls. The facade they've created when sober crumbles away under the influence. They become guilty of loving while intoxicated.

What if we dared to allow the Spirit within us to break down the barriers in our hearts? What if we welcomed the demolition

What if we dared to allow the Spirit within us to break down the barriers in our hearts?

of our walls so that what was really inside us flowed out? Instead of holding everything in, with control and fear, we could freely become the people God wants us to be—fully alive, fully real, fully capable of sharing our hearts.

6. They Don't Worry About Their Lives

When stress overwhelms some people, they pour a drink in order to forget their stress. And in that state of drunkenness, for a time, they forget that the mortgage is due, the job has been lost, their relationships are rocky.

As Christ followers, we have the Holy Spirit, always able to shoulder our worries, give us perspective, and grant us peace. Through prayer, we can lay out our stress for God to see, to sift, to remedy, or to give the ability to endure it with peace. So often, though, we run to substances or to ourselves when life spins on a crazy axis. Spirit-filled living empowers us to slay worry, give the management of our lives to Jesus, and rest in His embrace.

7. They Relish Being Out of Control

I watched my share of crazy parties when I was growing up, rampant with staggering adults, fights, and hazy rooms filled with passed-out people. People under the influence love to careen, to veer from normal behavior, even endangering themselves and others.

In Galatians Paul reminded us as Christ followers that we must be self-controlled. But that doesn't mean we live as control freaks. It means we relegate our sense of control to the Holy Spirit. And when He's at the helm of our lives, He careens us outside our comfort zones. He pushes us beyond our limits. He asks us to let go of what we think should happen for the sake of building the paradoxical kingdom of God—and often that looks strange. The question is, when others see us, do they see this kind of adventurous life? A life driven by our unpredictable God? Or are we clutching at control?

8. They Are Noticeable

In a crowd of sober people, a drunk person stands out. At a writers' conference, a group of writers enjoyed conversation outside our hotel. Two drunken newlyweds interrupted our halcyon evening, crashing into our conversation. We tried to talk to them, but they couldn't follow our line of reasoning, nor did they want to. They stumbled to another group of people, wreaking chaos as they stammered. Drunk folks are noticeable. People pick them out of a crowd.

So controlled by the love of God, our lives should be marked by hope, power, peace, grace, joy.

Similarly, as people who have been wildly redeemed by a beautiful God, we should stand out. But we should make a positive impression. So controlled by the love of God, our lives should be marked by hope, power, peace, grace, joy. In a sin-scarred world bent toward darkness, our well-lit lives should stand out. We may live in a night-like world, but as we follow Christ, that redemption within shines all the brighter on the darkened backdrop. Paul told us to live our lives so that we shine: "Live clean, innocent lives as children of God, shining like bright lights in a world full of crooked and perverse people" (Phil. 2:15 NLT).

• • •

It's nearly impossible to conjure up drunkenness. Although I had a few friends who would feign inebriation at parties, this kind of behavior is easily uncovered as fraudulent. In order to be drunk, one has to drink a lot. It's the same with our walk with Jesus. In order to live abandoned, Spirit-filled lives, we can't fake it. We can't examine what it looks like to be a Christian, then try those traits on for size. We can't imitate other believers; otherwise we're guilty of facade building. No. True transformation—genuine growth—comes when we drink deeply from the Fount of Blessing, from Jesus Christ through the Holy Spirit. We can't fake Him. He must be within us.

We need to be a noticeable people out of our own control, our hearts under Spirit-control. We should be addicted to the only person who can fill us—Jesus Christ who fully satisfies our thirst, who gives us everything we truly need to live this abundant life. It's not an accident that God sometimes places drunkenness and the Holy Spirit in the same sentence. That nearness is there to instruct us to so imbibe in the Holy Spirit within us that we dare to love others, live without walls, and become fully who God created us to be—dependent, surprising, infectious followers of Jesus Christ.

QUESTIONS FOR REFLECTION AND DISCUSSION

- *Looking back over the past year, when have you been authentic about your love for your family and friends? What made it easy to express your affection? When is it hard for you to share your love with others?*

- *What prejudices have you found in yourself when you meet a new person? How are those prejudices similar to your family of origin's?*

- *When was the last time you truly couldn't get enough of Jesus?*

- *How would it free you to let go of worrying about your reputation?*

- *What inhibits you from being truly on fire for Jesus right now?*

chapter Ten

Choose to Heal

The church doesn't do messy well.

—Susan Scheer[1]

SOMETIMES WHEN I CAN'T SLEEP, I MIND-WALK THROUGH houses from my childhood. As I survey the tiny white house, my home at ages five and six, I can't recall a single positive memory. I see those awful neighbor boys sexually abusing me. I remember my stolen tricycle. I smell marijuana, the plant that thrives under grow lights in the closet. As I strain my memory for something positive, I remember a friend I meet around the corner. She alone provides a positive memory.

The next house, a small pink-trimmed brown box, perplexes me. Still, I search the nooks and crannies for joy. Instead I find more drunken parties. A blood-stained hardwood floor concealed by an old oriental rug. Adults telling wide-eyed me that my home is haunted by angry ghosts. Again, I struggle for a memory to cherish. Eventually my mind skips to another friend, one across the busy street, whose mom makes me clothes and whose family takes me in. My new friend and her family fill my first and second grade years with rest.

I walk through a white house whose exterior paint peels like a bad sunburn. I live there from third to fifth grade. I see our horses, the ram-shackle barn with a chicken coop where the angry rooster lives. My biological father, divorced from my mom, doesn't live with me; his accidental death leaves me broken and wanting. My mom doesn't allow my grief, so my bedroom becomes a place of dark mourning—alone. I'm reprimanded for crying, so I muffle my tears in a pillow. And when I come home, I'm alone. I jimmy the lock on the back door of our house until it's set free, then I search for a snack in the emptiness. I can't think of a happy memory in all that meandering until I remember another friend, a sweet, lifelong friend who colors my life and brings laughter.

The farmhouse on acreage still looms big in my mind; its black shutters and white aluminum siding preen near the country road. A cedar tree, my shelter as I wait for my bus from sixth to tenth grade, stands guard to the right. My memories of this house include only me, caring for horses and animals and myself. Me, alone on ten acres, while my mom and stepdad work late, late, late. I learn to cook out of necessity. I contemplate suicide, despairing my isolated life. Yet a joyful memory rushes into me like grace-wind. I sit under a grand evergreen at Camp Timberlake, where I've just heard the most astounding words I'll ever hear, the glorious gospel of Jesus Christ. I realize I am not alone, not uncared for, not abandoned. I am loved.

The last childhood home I recount is my home during eleventh and twelfth grades. Oddly, I have little memory of that house, probably because I busied myself outside it most every day. I still can't abide split-level architecture, in part because of this home. My room is at the end of a hallway, and the door is often closed with me inside doing homework. A memory that sticks to my ribs is my Young Life leader, who tucks me under her wing, loves me, prays for me, and cheers for me. Another is my love for school and my deep desire to see my friends meet Jesus.

In the recollection, I realize something for the first time: all my positive memories occur outside the home—a friend, a family, another friend, a Young Life camp, my school. This underscores afresh that I grew up in a painful place, and the only way I could thrive was to leave what was supposed to be a haven (but failed to be) and search for my own haven in the arms and lives of others. This is my coping mechanism, one God uses to preserve me until the day He conquers my heart at fifteen.

The beautiful thing is that if a stranger met me today, she would not discern this story. God has so fully healed me from the past that most people have no idea about the devastation of my childhood. By God's sheer grace, they see joy, contentment, health, compassion, authenticity, and confidence. Not devastation. Not isolation. Not neglect. This is the power of Jesus to heal even the most broken life.

WOULD YOU LIKE TO GET WELL?

But what does healing have to do with growth? Aren't we to live in the Great Right Now, forgetting the past and moving toward the future? Why go back and mud-wrestle the past? Because Jesus asks us to. Just as He asked the lame man at the pool of Bethsaida, He asks us the same thing. Watch how Jesus interacted in John 5:6–9 (NLT):

> "Would you like to get well?"
>
> "I can't, sir," the sick man said, "for I have no one to put me into the pool when the water bubbles up. Someone else always gets there ahead of me."
>
> Jesus told him, "Stand up, pick up your mat, and walk!"
>
> Instantly, the man was healed!

The man didn't answer the question with a joyful, "Yes, absolutely, I want to get well." Instead he offered excuses, blaming others for his lack of healing. I wonder whether we do the same: "I'm messed up because of the way I was raised." "I can't

Why go back and mud-wrestle the past? Because Jesus asks us to.

change; this is how I'm wired. I'm just like my dad." "People keep re-injuring me, so what's the point of trying to be healthy?" It's easier to pass off our healing to another person, to blame others for our lack of spiritual health and growth. But Jesus didn't ask the people around the lame man, "Hey, why aren't you putting him in the water?" No, He directly addressed the lame man, the one who needed healing. And He does the same with you.

Would you like to get well?

Or would you rather be stuck, roped to the pain of the past? Yes, we are to look forward, but we cannot if our today is umbilically linked to our yesterday.

The nugget of this lame man's story is that Jesus didn't penalize the man for not answering His question. He didn't indulge his excuses. He simply commanded him to stand up. At that point the man had a choice—to stay rooted to the portico or to attempt the impossible and stand. He knew in his mind that he could not do this, but there must have been within him a tiny kernel of faith in Jesus' ability to do what He said He would do. So, where sinew once languished, and muscle atrophied, he dared to try. And in that trying, Jesus met him in his weakness and did for him what he was never able to do for himself. The man stood, then walked, then leaped. Then praised God.

THE HEART OF GOD IN OUR HEALING

The heart of God toward us mirrors this encounter. He asks us if we want to heal. We make excuses, or we're too afraid to believe we can be any different than who we are right now. We've made lameness our comfort zone, our happy normal. Still, He pesters us to stand. In that hesitant moment, we have a choice: to exert a tiny bit of faith in His ability, or to shrink back to our safe normal.

Do you know God wants you to live unshackled, freed from your past? Do you realize His love for you is steady and relentless? I'm not saying He desires for you to be happy or rich or wealthy or famous. One look at Jesus and how He walked the earth shows us this is a dangerous expectation for a Christ follower to have. Who are we to think we'll live any differently than Jesus who had no place to lay His head, who suffered hunger, whose fame waned and eventually contributed to His death? If we are His followers, we will follow in His steps, and that means we will suffer for His sake. But suffering for His sake is not the same thing as suffering from the wounds of our past.

Consider Joseph, who suffered extensively, and yet by God's grace he thrived after abandonment, wrongful accusation, and imprisonment. His past didn't dictate his future. Instead, his pain prepared him for that future in a unique way. He couldn't have been Pharaoh's right-hand man if he hadn't suffered the way he had. And if he let everything overwhelm and embitter him, I doubt he would've been elevated to that stately position. L. B. Cowman reflects on Joseph: "God never uses anyone to a great degree until he breaks the person completely. Joseph experienced more sorrow than the other sons of Jacob, and it led him into a ministry of food for the nations. For this reason, the Holy Spirit said of him, 'Joseph is a fruitful vine. . . . Near a spring, whose branches climb over a wall.'"[2]

We forget, don't we? That greatness rides on the shoulders of trials. We fail to remember that the burden of any injury is God's means for freedom and grace in our lives. It's okay to look back, to open wide the door to our past for the sake of healing. Not to dwell on. Not to obsess over or dismiss. Not to stay superglued to. But for the sake of divine healing. It's okay if you feel your heart can't heal. We humans are a frail lot, unable to enact something so big, so dynamic, so new. But we serve God, the Creator of all things, who knows us intimately, who fashioned us. He can take our brokenness and replace it

We fail to remember that the burden of any injury is God's means for freedom and grace in our lives.

with health. God uses injury in the past as the very means to bring us into new phases of growth.

Our past, whether it be yesterday, five years ago, or way back on the gritty sidewalks of our childhood, can be redeemed. God is sovereign even over our heart-healing process. He may not instantly heal us as He did the lame man. Sometimes healing takes months and years. But God gives us so much in the process, even when we feel like we're cornered in darkness.

HEALING IN THE WARDROBE

The healing journey is like facing the Narnian wardrobe. The circumstances of your life and the behaviors you can't seem to overcome are like the guests in *The Lion, the Witch and the Wardrobe*, stalking the old house while the Pevensie kids flee. Either they stay and suffer the consequences, or they venture into the wardrobe. And in that wardrobe, past fur coats and old ladies' garments, the icy wind of Narnia and the pine smell of the wooded world lure the kids inward. Once they've committed to Narnia (Edmund notwithstanding), they embark on an entirely new journey that will change them from the inside out and readjust the way they look at the outside world. God-initiated healing is that way. He brings us, if we dare, to a new place, but it's not a familiar place. And in that outside-of-our-comfort-zone spot, He woos our attention, shows us our past in light of His viewpoint, and sets us back on our feet again to have new adventures.

Yet we tend to be a shortchanging culture, desiring the adventurous life on the other side without first having to face the wardrobe. God ever beckons us to the new land precisely because He knows what lies on the other end: healing, health, joy, a new perspective.

It takes courage to enter the wardrobe. Why? Because examining the past can be hard. In the crucible of that place, Jesus grabs our hand, sits beside us, and watches as the movies of our past flicker before us.

He cries with us. He laughs alongside us. Although it is painful and black, He is always there. When we finish the movie and the credits roll across the screen (He is the credits!), He leads us through the icy world to the green at the other end—the rejuvenated Narnia. New vistas welcome us. We see things we've never seen before. We experience life in such a way that life on the previous side of the wardrobe seems smaller, less important. Freed from bitterness and anger, we walk forward, healed.

But many of us falter as we place our big toe in the wardrobe's bowels. We shrink back, more afraid of what we'll see on the other side of the threshold than what God can do. We expect to gain victory and growth without struggle or pain. Nothing worth grasping, in terms of growth and health, is cheap in God's economy. It cost God everything—including His life. It will cost us to heal. It will hurt. And often the rehabilitation is harder than the injury itself. But the result of a changed, healed life is worth the cost of taking the first scary step through.

Nothing worth grasping, in terms of growth and health, is cheap in God's economy.

Some of you reading this may be thinking, *Well, that's fine for you, but I can handle my life just fine. I don't need to heal.* As gently as I can write, I remind you that in your own strength, you won't heal. Pushing down the past won't make you heal. Pretending it didn't happen won't heal you. We can't heal from unreality. We all have skeletons, injuries, regrets. We can't deny them. But we can take them as an offering to the Lord and let Him have free rein over all those painful moments.

You still may be thinking, *I am managing. How I am on the inside doesn't affect others around me anyway.* That's not true. Remember that Jesus reminded the Pharisees that what is inside our hearts can't help but overflow into our lives. What lives in there comes out. And it will eventually affect others.

Consider the toll your past is taking on the ones you love. Ask God to heal your heart for the sake of your children, your spouse, the people in your life.

So if you can't walk through the wardrobe for your own sake, consider the toll your past is taking on the ones you love. Ask God to heal your heart for the sake of your children, your spouse, the people in your life. Spend some time this week asking God to show you where your past is affecting your today. If you're brave, ask those closest to you how your reaction to the past affects your actions right now. Then repent; ask forgiveness of those you've hurt. Ask God to lead you into your Narnia. Like the lame man, stand up and walk there, even if it means you have to limp. Trust that God is big enough to shoulder every single pain and burden and injury you've ever experienced. Surrender your heart, your life, your will to Him. Let Him have His healing way with you. Hold tightly to His hand. Then wait in anticipation for the healing, the new vista, the renewed life, the genuine growth.

THE "THAT'S IT" MENTALITY

While it's easy for me to write this admonishment to you, it's much harder to follow in my life. Often I'm guilty of a "that's it" mentality when it comes to healing. I'll slog my way through another wardrobe, admire the vista on the other side, then think, *Finally! That's it! I'm finished healing.* Then something new crops up. Initially this causes me to despair. But soon I realize the Lord is a gentleman healer. He reveals our needs and broken places when we can handle them, and He gently leads us as a kind shepherd leads his sheep, toward healing.

At this moment, He uses my younger daughter as a proof text of an ancient wound. She told me she hurt her leg at school, and she limped to prove it. But she kept switching legs, and I grew impatient, trying to be empathetic, yet not enabling her. Together we watched the movie adaptation of *The Secret Life of Bees*. And as I sat there, the Lord chatted with me about my mother wound. Lily, a motherless girl, said, "You can tell which girls lack mothers by the look of their hair."[3] I remembered my hair as a girl, often tangled, never braided. Once my mom grew so frustrated with the beehive of a mess that she took me to a barber and had it all hacked off. So much so that I looked like a boy, and kids teased me at school. This memory opened up a hole in my heart. In all these years, I've come to the conclusion that a girl never outgrows her need for a nurturing mother. I've had to die to my desire to have one.

Lily, the main character, abandoned by her mother, lived under the shadow of that neglect. At one point, she grabbed fresh jars of honey and hurled them against a wall in a rage. As she did this, my limping daughter Julia said, "I love this movie, but I don't like this part." She closed her eyes, then opened them after the jars ceased flying.

I watched, fully understanding Lily's wrath. I remembered how my mom seemed put out by me, how "in the way" I felt around her. She told me she never wanted another child because apparently I'd been enough to bother with. In light of that feeling of being wholly unwanted, I spent my childhood trying to be unnoticed, suppressing my needs, or acting out in order to garner attention. None of it worked. The attention seldom came.

Julia walked away from me after the movie with her limp. It continued to come and go, depending on whether I watched her or not. And over the next few days, I noticed myself getting angrier and angrier about it. I knew it was a ploy for attention, which poked at me.

I talked to God about the intermittent limp. Should I confront Julia about it? Do I share a bit of what I did as a child and try to figure out why she wants attention? As I threw my questions skyward, I sensed God say, *Her limp is not about her; it's about you.* I let those words sink into me. He was right. When I watched her limp, I saw myself way back when, desperately trying to get attention, yet failing. I despised the young me in that moment. How dare I have needs? How dare I try to meet them? Aren't I better off numbing myself? Making myself unremarkable? Hiding my hurts so I don't pester?

I surrendered again as God placed another wardrobe door before me. He wanted to heal this part of my heart that despised my neediness. He wanted me to come through to the other side so I could offer empathy to Julia, come alongside her, and discern why she was feeling needy. His healing in this instance was for her sake. She needed a mom who was present, selfless, and interested. His healing was also for my sake because it wasn't healthy to live in reaction to past wounds, nor was it healthy for my heart to despise myself as a child.

My week flashed before me, and I saw how easily I slipped into neglect as a mom—my fallback, what was modeled to me in the past. I didn't want to duplicate my childhood, so I asked God again to fill, heal, and forgive me for living life in my own strength and agenda this week.

Growth happens solely from the inside out. We can't decorate our outsides, creating impeccable facades, feigning growth.

Like you, I want to grow beyond this. I want to change. I want to be present for my kids, but that involves a change of heart, not merely an external change of actions. So I asked God for help, then I spent some good time with Julia, hearing her, listening to her heart. And as she walked away from me, her limp vanished.

Growth happens solely from the inside out. We can't decorate our outsides, creating impeccable facades, feigning growth. Our hearts must first be healed by the only One who can heal, and then our splendor will radiate from within. Then the growth will flourish. But we can't have it the other way around.

• • •

We must see our penchant to stuff our pain and subconsciously live in reaction to that pain as evidence of an atrophied heart. Jesus wants to heal us. He wants to walk into those wardrobes with us. He wants us to be so fully healed today that no one would think we had a painful past. That's part of the beauty of the gospel, this holy rejuvenation, God taking the broken parts of ourselves and remaking them into something different. We die to our wounds so that He can resurrect newness of life, joy, and connectedness with others.

We hand Him our bitterness, and He holds the reasons for the bitterness, scatters that bitterness to the wind, and replaces it with gratitude and a willingness to risk in relationship again.

Jesus wastes none of our stories, even our tales of woe. He transforms them into epic adventures where we dare to face our past for the sake of our present.

That's the goal of healing—engagement in this life. Our suffering, then, serves as a catalyst for new growth and inside-out living. Psalm 119:71 confirms this: "My suffering was good for me, for it taught me to pay attention to your decrees" (NLT). Jesus wastes none of our stories, even our tales of woe. He transforms them into epic adventures where we dare to face our past for the sake of our present. He changes our hearts, cleanses our sin, and loves us too much to let us stay chained to the pain. He wants to heal us, and as with the lame man, He beckons us, knowing we need healing to pave the way for new growth. Looking into our eyes, our souls, He asks, "Would you like to get well?"

QUESTIONS FOR REFLECTION AND DISCUSSION

- *If Jesus stood before you today and asked if you'd like to get well, how would you respond?*

- *What aspects of your past do you find yourself overthinking or reliving?*

- *In what ways has the past affected the way you live today?*

- *Have you seen how injury in the past has affected your relationships today? How?*

- *Where are you with the wardrobe? Have you stepped inside? Gone to the other side? Afraid to go in? Why or why not?*

Chapter Eleven

Lean into Brokenness

No one will gain all without having lost all.

—Madame Guyon[1]

Today on my run, I look behind me to see the orange-orbed sun pink the sky. Before me stretch several telephone poles, lining the street like cross-shaped sentries. As I pass them, the song playing on my iPod is about the cross, brokenness, shame, and victory. The coincidence isn't lost on me. Why do growth and strength and wherewithal grow when parts of us die? Why do we think it should be different for us? Why do we gravitate toward success first, not realizing that the most beautiful victories in the kingdom of God happen after humiliation? Brokenness? Despair? That's the power of the cross. It's the mystery of the gospel. That clay-footed people like us could experience genuine life from our losses so that our boasting will be in God's capability to move in and through us, not our ability to live this life well. I love how Paul put it:

> Remember, dear brothers and sisters, that few of you were wise in the
> world's eyes or powerful or wealthy when God called you. Instead,

God chose things the world considers foolish in order to shame those who think they are wise. And he chose things that are powerless to shame those who are powerful. God chose things despised by the world, things counted as nothing at all, and used them to bring to nothing what the world considers important. As a result, no one can ever boast in the presence of God. (1 Cor. 1:26–29 NLT)

Our desperation points others to Jesus' inspiration inside us. We are pressed and hemmed in so that we stop our addiction to control and relinquish that control to God. Paul again reassured us of the beauty of brokenness when he told the Corinthian believers,

We think you ought to know, dear brothers and sisters, about the trouble we went through in the province of Asia. We were crushed and overwhelmed beyond our ability to endure, and we thought we would never live through it. In fact, we expected to die. But as a result, we stopped relying on ourselves and learned to rely only on God, who raises the dead. And he did rescue us from mortal danger, and he will rescue us again. We have placed our confidence in him, and he will continue to rescue us. (2 Cor. 1:8–10 NLT)

A broken person understands she needs rescue, and she depends on God to resurrect and deliver. And she also understands that even if God chooses not to deliver, His ways are higher and more amazing than what we can fathom. Shadrach, Meshach, and Abednego of Old Testament furnace fame understood this when they replied to the king: "King Nebuchadnezzar, we do not need to defend ourselves before you in this matter. If we are thrown into the blazing furnace, the God we serve is able to deliver us from it, and he will deliver us from Your Majesty's hand. But even if he does not, we want you to know, Your Majesty, that we will not serve your gods or worship the image of gold you have set up" (Dan. 3:16–18 UPDATED NIV). That's obedient brokenness.

SHEEP OR GOATS?

I experienced this kind of obedience as a carful of us bumbled over rocky paths in northern Ghana. The driver turned on his headlights as dusk faded to night. Sitting in the front seat, I spied a group of goats reclining on the road in front of us. The driver honked. They startled, then milled away. I asked about the goats, and the man said, "They are both sheep and goats." Because the sheep looked exactly like goats, I was puzzled. Usually sheep are fluffy, but not these. He sensed my confusion. "You can tell the difference between a sheep and a goat very simply," he said. "The goats have tails that point to the sky. They are proud, these goats. But the sheep lay their tails toward the earth. They are more timid." I thought of the connection between Jesus' parable of the end of this age, how the sheep head heavenward and the goats face a downward punishment, the opposite direction their tails point.

It's the same for us in Jesus' paradoxical kingdom where the poor find wealth and the last find the first seat. There is no room for the stiff-necked. And God is far, far away from those who refuse to bend their tails to the earth, whose hearts remain hard.

We look at those Pharisees and refuse to see ourselves in them.

Jesus had much to say about the hard-hearted, often pointing His judgment to the whitewashed Pharisees. But we look at those Pharisees and refuse to see ourselves in them. We gaze at Pharaoh and his proud, hard heart and surmise that he was bad and we'd never be like him. We would rather live in the land of lying to ourselves than truly see our state before a holy God.

This kind of attitude typifies those who will be outside the New Jerusalem: "Outside the city are the dogs—the sorcerers, the sexually immoral, the murderers, the idol worshipers, and all who love to live a lie" (Rev. 22:15 NLT). That last phrase stops me short every time, "all who love to live a lie." We are self-deceived folks with wicked hearts bent toward selfishness, hearts that resist selflessness. We would rather live a lie than come to the Truth Personified, Jesus, and let Him show us our hearts. It's when we isolate ourselves from Him, choosing to live independent lives, that our hearts harden. Only when we return, in a state of repentance, will we experience a true softening. In that place, we'll naturally live humble lives.

The Dinner Party

Jesus gave good advice when He told a story about a dinner party (Luke 14:7–11). He warned us against taking the most important seat at a banquet because the host might demote us. Instead, we're to take the last seat. In doing so, we might be promoted, but we'll have no expectations of that. He warned, "Those who exalt themselves will be humbled, and those who humble themselves will be exalted" (Luke 14:11 NLT). We must take the last seat, to prefer humility over honor. In that humble place, we experience God's lifting.

Brokenness is the avenue for God to work. It's His welcome party. Paul, too, realized this avenue. Read his words in the J. B. Phillips translation:

> So tremendous, however, were the revelations that God gave me that, in order to prevent my becoming absurdly conceited, I was given a physical handicap—one of Satan's angels—to harass me and effectually stop any conceit. Three times I begged the Lord for it to leave me, but his reply has been, "My grace is enough for you: for where there is weakness, my power is shown the more completely." Therefore, *I have cheerfully made up my mind to be proud of my weaknesses*, because they mean a deeper experience of the power of Christ. I can even enjoy weaknesses, suffering, privations, persecutions and difficulties for Christ's sake. For my very weakness makes me strong in him. (2 Cor. 12:9–10, emphasis mine)

Paul, by his own will, chose to be cheerful about his weakness. Talk about countercultural! We spend lifetimes decorating over our weaknesses, hoping no one sees them, yet Paul was proud of them. Why? Because in that state of broken weakness, he experienced more of Jesus. We are nearer to the heart of God when we break.

THE BEAUTY OF THE BROKEN PARTS

What if our self-sufficient lives gave way to self-forgetfulness and God awareness? What if we lived in anticipation of what God would do through our broken parts rather than spend years trying to repair the breaches in our lives? What if we embraced the radical truth that God is clearly seen through our cracks, not our smooth facades? How would this world look if we dared to believe such a paradox?

God breaks us for better things.

God breaks us for better things. In daily life I experience this. In my writing journey, full of rejection and never-seen toiling, I understand this. As I parent my children, I know this. I must be broken to be reshaped. I must be cracked before the repair. And the repair, painful as it is, makes God stronger in me. God presses me toward brokenness because He loves me, but the converse is also true. I can choose to live a broken life out of my affection for Him. It's the gift He loves to receive from His followers, not because He's bent on our destruction, but because He knows we're happiest when we're most dependent on Him.

• • •

Ever wonder why God didn't give us everything we needed in ourselves? He knew we needed to find fulfillment in something bigger than ourselves: Him. Unfortunately we've believed the lie that fulfillment comes in two human forms only: in perfecting ourselves, or finding others who will fill the holes in our lives. Some people spend lifetimes pursuing one or both, experiencing disappointment, disillusionment, and despair. Instead of using that sadness to give up and bow our "tails" beneath us, we buck up and try harder, and as we do, our hearts harden. We get angry that God gave us limitations or that He made "those people" so awful so as to hurt us so badly. We blame God for the very things meant to glue us to Him.

Why not, instead, see those limitations as God's gentle wooing? He is our Creator. We, the created. Who better knows how to love, forgive, enervate, and establish us than our Creator? The limitations He sends are invitations to His heart, His ways, His abundance.

> The limitations He sends are invitations to His heart, His ways, His abundance.

God's heart for us is that we would need Him; we'd lay our heads on His chest like a child needing a daddy after skinning a knee. We cannot experience this kind of relationship with Him if we are like those Ghana goats, tails proud. We cannot grow to be more like Jesus without brokenness. Ironic, isn't it? To grow, we give up. We rest. We give God control. Oswald Chambers wrote, "I am called to live in perfect relation to God so that my life produces a longing after God in other lives, not admiration for myself. Thoughts about myself hinder my usefulness to God. God is not after perfecting me to be a specimen in His showroom; He is getting me to the place where He can use me. Let Him do what He likes."[2] That's the truth. God uses humble sheep to do His work.

QUESTIONS FOR REFLECTION AND DISCUSSION

- *In what ways have you identified with a Ghana goat? A sheep?*

- *Why is it hard to take the last seat?*

- *What is the correlation between being broken and growth in your life?*

- *Why do you think God uses the foolish things of this world to shame the wise?*

- *Why do you think we all struggle with self-deception?*

BE KIND TO YOURSELF

This is the very perfection of a man, to find out his own imperfection.

—SAINT AUGUSTINE[1]

SHE KNEW SHE SAID MEAN THINGS TO PEOPLE. SHE acknowledged the shock factor of her words. But she couldn't see why those words and her pattern of bullying others were any sort of problem. "I'm authentic," she told me. "I tell people exactly what I'm thinking in the moment." I tried to help her realize the direct correlation between her mean behavior and others' reactions, but she contented herself to stay blinded. Although she may have been self-aware enough to know she hurt people, that awareness didn't morph into holy introspection or life change.

My husband and I, after several years in ministry, have come to this conclusion: the hallmark of growth in a Christian's life is self-awareness. Not the kind of awareness where we vaguely acknowledge that we sometimes sin, but the ability to take a soul inventory with a view toward growth.

Two people reveal the need for self-awareness.

From the outside, Kyle appeared to be everything a Christian man should be. He had a good family and a dedicated wife, and he worked full time in ministry. He preferred to keep his heart far away from the people he ministered to, and he seldom shared a struggle with the members of his ministry team. In community, fissures opened. Others around him saw his anger, prejudices, greed, and control. When confronted about these issues, Kyle lashed out, pushing away and denying the problems. Eventually he moved on because of his unwillingness to acknowledge and deal with his issues.

Steve, by contrast, invested in a small group of men who challenged him to open up. Though it was not easy at first, he eventually realized that his anger issues stemmed from some childhood experiences he hadn't yet fully explored. The men in his group challenged him to rethink his responses, hard advice to welcome. Over the next few months, Steve started changing. His anger lessened. He became more patient. Instead of viewing community as pesky and tiresome, he realized that true growth happened in that context. Ironic, since self-awareness had to do with the self, when really it stemmed from the watchful hearts and eyes of others who helped him deal with his issues squarely and bravely.

Growth comes when we dare to be brave enough to see ourselves, then ask why our hearts bend toward sinful ways.

Both men could say they were self-aware, but only one grew as a result.

None of us like to see ourselves as flawed, broken people. We hate to see our shortcomings. But growth comes when we dare to be brave enough to see ourselves, then ask why our hearts bend toward sinful ways.

The *Examen*

Saint Ignatius Loyola perfected a method known as the *examen*, where he looked at his life at noon and the end of the day to see whether he was walking well with Jesus. He examined (tested) how he lived, but with gratitude. Consider these five steps of the examen:

1. *Become aware of God's presence.* How many times do you look back over your days and realize you didn't invite Jesus into them? It's easy to live robotic—doing tasks, meeting obligations, attending to things—and forget that the God of the universe wants to walk alongside you in everything. Slowing down a moment helps you sense God's nearness.

2. *Review the day with gratitude.* We tend to look back on our days and harshly evaluate our actions. To learn to review a day with gratitude doesn't come naturally, but it's entirely necessary and a large part of becoming self-aware. Ask yourself, What made me grateful today? What blessed me?

3. *Pay attention to your emotions.* Emotions are the gateway to growth. When were you angry? Happy? Irritated? Unfulfilled? Worried? Discovering your emotions, then asking yourself why, is an important part of growth. If you're daring, ask your spouse or a good friend to help you identify your emotions from the day.

4. *Choose one feature of the day and pray from it.* It's usually easiest to find the stress point of your day and use that to spur your prayer life. If you were frustrated at work, ask God to give you patience. If a child exasperated you, pray for her heart.

5. *Look toward tomorrow.*[2] Having a future-oriented perspective, realizing that every day is a new one, full of possibilities and grace and do-overs, will revolutionize your growth. Sometimes we get so stuck in the pain of today or the sting of yesterday that we fail to anticipate the future. Yet God beckons us always forward, onward, and upward.

If it's not easy for you to practice self-awareness, make this an area of prayer. Ask those closest to you to help you figure out where you're stuck. Often others can see your blind spots and can gently help you recognize your areas of weakness and sin. When others come alongside you, and you humbly welcome feedback, your growth multiplies. The side effect will be the opposite of what you anticipate. You may fear that authenticity about your faults will make you less in people's eyes, but the inverse tends to be true. People like to be around other flawed folks. They're drawn to real people who admit their mistakes. It makes others feel less alone.

WHAT ABOUT THOSE OF US WHO BEAT OURSELVES UP?

In all this, beware of self-awareness taken to the extreme. Once, a mature Christian friend gave me a diagnosis: overactive conscience. He said my conscience worked overtime, preferring to berate me for my flaws. A healthy conscience helps us say no to bad things and confess to others when we've wronged them, but an overactive one invents things to apologize for. Once I heard his words, I knew he spoke the truth about me. I'm so aware of my faults that I analyze and dissect them, place them before far too many people, hit myself over the heart with my worthlessness, and say all sorts of mean things to myself. I've shared this with others long enough now to know that I'm not the only one who struggles with this.

God and I are in the process of changing this, but it's not easy to loose myself from a forty-four-year-old pattern. I'm held back by the rut I've created with my words whispered to myself over a lifetime. Words like, "You'll never be enough. Never do enough. Never achieve enough." Beyond those words, which I've learned to quiet more and more, worse words scream at me the moment I feel guilty. Words like these:

- "You should have . . ."
- "Why didn't you . . . ?"
- "You've really messed up this time."
- "You will never overcome this sin. It's part of you now. It's written in stone."
- "Because you did/thought this, you are unworthy of God's love."

I feel gut pain when I read the words I've spoken over myself, how I've abused myself. I treat myself like a criminal. I've been guilty of "shoulding" all over myself. And sometimes I think I'd treat a criminal much, much better. I'm the victim of myself, of my overactive conscience. I feel bad for things I didn't do or intend. I can't seem to touch, to feel, to receive Jesus' wild, affectionate love. I want to change.

If you're plagued by this, do you want to be set free? Growth comes from freedom. But what does it look like? Here's what freedom and growth might look like:

- When you mess up, you offer yourself grace, the same grace you offer others when they wrong you.
- You silence the angry words directed your way by simply saying, "Jesus loves me."
- You live in a deeper level of freedom and joy because you no longer believe in your deep unworthiness.
- You have more moments in life when you feel genuine elation, rejoicing in the outrageous grace of Jesus.
- You forgive others as you revel in the sheer volume of how much God has forgiven you.
- You no longer take responsibility for others' sins.
- You truly believe God has removed your sin as far as the east and the west, then joyfully live accordingly.
- You smile more.
- The static anger in your head quiets, replaced by the affectionate words of the Almighty.

To grow is to be free from the tyranny of your heart. Joyful. Alive. Reveling in Jesus' love. But you can't do that when you listen to your berating. Why do we tend to love everyone else, offering grace and forgiveness aplenty to others, but we cannot extend that same grace to ourselves? Once, when I let my husband in on the angry voices in my head, he shook his own and said, "Mary, I would never talk to you that way. Why are you abusing yourself?" Then I realized how awful I'd been to me, how little regard I had for my heart and life. Through that I learned (slowly) how to identify when I lapsed into overactive conscience mode. Here are three things that helped me:

1. *Listen to the correct voice.* The voice of the enemy of our souls condemns us without restraint, making us feel like we'll never amount to anything. It's then that we recognize that voice and choose to ignore it or replace it with the truth.
2. *Remember: when God convicts, it's always with hope.* If your conscience is screaming, there is little hope involved. You'll feel like you'll never overcome a sin. But when God convicts, grace and peace and a huge dose of hope are heaped on. When He convicts me, I feel a holy aha and an underlying sense that He loves me and will empower me to change.
3. *Trust your friends.* When I'm tormented and beating myself up over a sin, I can immediately know if my conscience is hyperactive by sharing it with a friend. Friends give us good perspective and are better able to discern if something is worthy of repentance or simply must be let go.

A passage in 1 John has helped me walk through this issue: "This then is how we know that we belong to the truth, and how we set our hearts at rest in his presence whenever our hearts condemn us. For God is greater than our hearts, and he knows everything. Dear friends, if our hearts do not condemn us, we have confidence before God and receive from him anything we ask, because we obey his commands and do what pleases him" (3:19–23 NIV).

I've always thought of being overly self-examining as a true mark of humility. Somehow, I felt if I were super hard on myself, God would smile down upon me. *Good girl,* I thought He would say. *You know you are made from dust. I'm so glad you are beating yourself up! Way to go on your trek to being humble.*

How wrong I was! This verse confirms it: "Take My yoke upon you and learn from Me, for I am gentle and humble in heart, and you will find rest for your souls" (Matt. 11:29 NASB). Jesus says He is humble. And I resonate with that. After all, He left the glory of heaven to walk our dusty streets. For one moment of excruciating time, He stepped out of the dance of the Trinity so He could be humbly obedient and spare us God the Father's wrath. He sacrificed comfort and relationship so we could have God's comfort and relationship. All because of humility.

Why do we tend to love everyone else, offering grace and forgiveness aplenty to others, but we cannot extend that same grace to ourselves?

The wrench thrown in my errant theology was this: Jesus was sinless. He didn't spend time beating Himself up about His sin because He didn't have any. And yet, He is the picture of humility. Besides that, God the Father sees us through the lens of Jesus. Humility is not about beating ourselves up; it's about understanding the amazing nature of Jesus. It shifts our thinking from being defensive to becoming proactive. From retaliating against ourselves to becoming more like Jesus: obedient and rejoicing.

It's about hanging with Jesus, about being with Him to discover what humility is and isn't. His promise in the Matthew verse is this: if we do that, if we lean into Jesus and His notions of humility, we will find rest for our souls. I used to think that rest had to do with a general feeling of peace, but now as I read that verse, I see that rest is feeling like it's okay to live in my own skin. It's peace with tyrannical, perfectionist me. Jesus frees me from my overcritical self.

In that, we can resonate even more with Paul's words: "To me it is a very small thing that I may be examined by you, or by any human court;

in fact, I do not even examine myself. For I am conscious of nothing against myself, yet I am not by this acquitted; but the one who examines me is the Lord" (1 Cor. 4:3–4 NASB);

He didn't spend time beating Himself up about His sin because He didn't have any. And yet, He is the picture of humility.

and "The faith which you have, have as your own conviction before God. Happy is he who does not condemn himself in what he approves" (Rom. 14:22 NASB). It's not our job to relentlessly examine ourselves. It's our job to learn from Jesus, to hear His words sung over our lives. He is the One who examines. If we want to be "happy" as Paul said, we must be strong in our personal convictions, but not so much that we can't exercise them without fear of what others will think or what our critical hearts will think.

Mike Mason speaks to this issue in his book *Practicing the Presence of People*:

When it comes to guilt and condemnation, we should all regard ourselves as alcoholics. One little sip of the stuff goes straight to our heads and we lose all perspective. In our younger days, perhaps, the effects of our addiction didn't seem so ravaging. We thought we could handle it. But now the dragon has caught up with us. We have a progressive, fatal illness for which there is only one cure: Don't take that first drink! Stay away from condemnation! One sip ruins our freedom.[3]

May it be that we understand that living like Jesus means not taking a sip of that self-condemnation cup!

• • •

Which brings us back to the beginning of this chapter: self-awareness. There's a big difference between being aware of our sinful tendencies and berating ourselves relentlessly. Neglect has no self-awareness at all.

Balance exercises self-awareness. Condemnation comes from giving in to a hyperactive conscience. Paul instructed us to examine ourselves: "Examine yourselves to see if your faith is genuine. Test yourselves. Surely you know that Jesus Christ is among you; if not, you have failed the test of genuine faith" (2 Cor. 13:5 NLT). So it's wise and right to do so, but we must avoid overanalyzing ourselves to the point of extreme condemnation. Because Paul refreshed us with this truth: "There is therefore now no condemnation for those who are in Christ Jesus" (Rom. 8:1).

Because of Jesus Christ, we are free.

QUESTIONS FOR REFLECTION AND DISCUSSION

- *Why is self-awareness important? When in your life have you been self-aware in a healthy way? When have you been oblivious?*

- *In your own words, define an overactive conscience. Do you struggle with this? Do you know someone who does?*

- *What statements have you spoken over your life that have condemned you or hurt you? Write them out. Ask a friend to evaluate whether they're true.*

- *How does realizing Jesus didn't live with an overactive conscience help you today?*

- *When was the last time God convicted you about a particular sin? What happened after He did so?*

Hands—How We Live

JESUS DIDN'T MERELY SAY HE LOVED THIS WORLD. HE stretched out His hands on the cross in order to save it from its own tyranny. He incarnated into human flesh, which means He forever walks the universe with eyes, feet, hands.

With those hands He blessed and healed lepers. He touched demoniacs. He welcomed friends. He pushed over tables. With this earth's dirt beneath His fingernails, He prayed bread and fish would feed multitudes. He stooped low and washed feet. He served, leaving us all an example.

With minds aright, hearts renewed, we can use our hands as Jesus did—to serve others, to love well, to dirty ourselves in the needs of this world. To the extent that we see this world as Jesus sees it, then act on His injunction to love others, we become more like Him.

In this section we'll examine our hands, how we spend our money, battle spiritual darkness, and live our lives each day. We'll rework our view of failure. We'll find out how to grow side by side instead of in isolation. We'll look at some entirely different disciplines and discern the importance of following in Jesus' footsteps (handprints).

RELINQUISH MONEY

The love of money is the root of all kinds of evil. And some
people, craving money, have wandered from the true
faith and pierced themselves with many sorrows.

—1 TIMOTHY 6:10 NLT

COLLEGE LOOMED OVER ME, EVEN THEN. AFTER WE RETURNED from overseas, our daughter would spend four and a half years finishing her basic education, and then college would rear its undergrad head and demand to be fed. Its hunger growled at me. At first, I had this supernatural sense of God's provision. When we lost our home to a con man and foreclosure loomed, the Lord asked me a simple question: "Do you believe I own the cattle on a thousand hills or don't you?" (Ps. 50:10). For several days I wrestled with His ownership, knowing all good Christians ought to believe this truth, but realizing I'd given it lip service, not heart service.

Eventually after much teeth grinding, I exhaled, "Yes, Lord, I now believe You own everything." I practiced the art of relinquishment then, and the peace that followed astounded me.

- No more worrying about our budget (though I still worked to manage it well on foreign soil).
- No more late nights wrangling numbers and wringing my hands in worry.
- No more scheming as to how we'd make more mammon.

In that space of relinquishment, I set up a new paradigm, one of fretlessness.

But back in the States, the worry insisted on needling me. The hard-won peace dissipated each year college drew nearer. Although I would, at times, remember God's provision of the past (we'd survived foreclosure as missionaries on support!), I spent more time worrying about money. That worry became my mantra, my filter, the stagnation of my growth. Because, as Jesus aptly put it, you can't serve God and the money god. And in my quest to fill college's coffers, I'd worshipped far too long at the feet of the money deity. With Sophie such a strong student, we prayed for scholarships, but their elusiveness kept me cinched to worry.

WORRY ABOUT MONEY EQUALS DISTRUST

We can justify our money worries. I know. I'm quite adept at it. But underneath is a canker of distrust that God can't provide our needs. (Note that I didn't say *our wants*.) In this state of faithlessness, I choose not to believe He is a wise, giving, all-knowing Father who notices when sparrows fall or the hair on my head renumbers itself. I become like those pesky Israelites, forgetting the providential hand of God. I become chummy with Peter, looking more at the waves of worry than the clear eyes of Jesus. I don't look any different from those who don't follow Christ, blending into the stress-laden culture around me, more concerned about my crumbling kingdom than in building the kingdom of God with my sweat equity.

During this phase of my life, which I'm embarrassed to share, I expended my energy thinking of ways to make my writing career lucrative (insert laugh track here). I put my hands to marketing, public relations, social media. I found mentors who pushed me toward branding and trained me to speak on the radio in such a way so as to bring in more contacts and more money. Though I learned a lot during this tutelage, I didn't like what I became. I veered dangerously close to a multilevel marketing pest, viewing people not as those whom Jesus died for, but as folks who could further my message, buy my book, or employ me to speak.

I offered my reputation and my soul on the altar of worry.

I held tightly to my career, but my career didn't pay me back because what we grasp irrevocably binds us to it. When Jesus spoke with the rich young ruler, He found the man's heart tight-fisting money. He asked the man to hand it all over, but the man couldn't. He walked away grieved, his hands full, his heart empty.

I have the rich young ruler's DNA, bent toward money, which ultimately means I want to be my own provision. But God graciously brought me to the end of myself and my career when I realized I'm ultimately not running this show. Either I can choose to keep pushing, viewing people as commodities and running myself into burnout, or I can relinquish.

He Does Own the Cattle on a Thousand Hills

When I realized my predicament, God again asked me, "Do you believe I own the cattle on a thousand hills?"

This time I hemmed and hawed months instead of days. I lived as if I didn't believe God owned it all. I wrestled with relinquishment. I argued with God, begged Him at times, reminded Him about college and how very much it cost. His silence answered.

Finally I shook hands with relinquishment and gave it all back to Jesus. I realized it's not my job to provide for college. It's not my job to run my life. It's not my job to fret. It's not my job to force writing to become lucrative. It's my job to relinquish control, to trust God for money, and to have an open hand. I wrote this scripture in my journal: "God is opposed to the proud, but gives grace to the humble" (1 Peter 5:5 NASB).

Trust in your instinct that says [God] will provide for you.

Then I wrote, "I'm acting proud when I think I am the sole provision for Sophie's college education. Forgive me for not being humble and dependent. Forgive me for worry."

That's when the Lord spoke to me again, His sweet, beautiful voice echoing through me: *Go back to that place of dependence. Trust in your instinct that says I will provide for you. Don't let anyone or any circumstance persuade you to worry again.*

So I fought my way back to peace, reclaiming the years I lost to worry. I chose to believe God's provision, and my heart found rest.

That rest was the cake and the icing, too, but God saw fit to add a cherry on top. Sophie received a letter from the college she would attend, awarding her its largest scholarship, a full tuition ride. In that moment, I could hear God's holy laughter. He who knew it all along must've watched in amusement as I tried-tried-tried to make something happen that didn't even need to happen. God had it planned all along, and all my worry just led me in knot-tying circles.

GROWTH COMES IN LETTING GO

We learn relinquishment the hard way, but it's absolutely necessary for strong, sustainable growth. It's a choice we make every day to open our hand when our fist is tight, and it often means opening our wallets, letting them stand bare before the God who owns the cattle on a thousand hills. It's been said that the last thing to be converted in a Christian's life is that stingy wallet. In this age of digital banking, our online register registers more about our hearts than any other holy action we may tout. Simply put: crazy growth comes when we realize God's ownership.

I love how Eugene Peterson renders Matthew 6:19–21, the famous words of Jesus about treasures and heaven: "Don't hoard treasure down here where it gets eaten by moths and corroded by rust or—worse!—stolen by burglars. Stockpile treasure in heaven, where it's safe from moth and rust and burglars. It's obvious, isn't it? The place where your treasure is, is the place you will most want to be, and end up being" (MSG). Working for the sake of trinkets on earth is futility, as nothing here will last. What will last is what is eternal, those things we do (such as believing God will take care of us, blessing my readers instead of seeing them as commodities, resting in God's ownership of everything in my life) that make God smile and bring rest to our souls. Money is a cheap but powerful substitute for Jesus, and wielding money is intoxicating, but it won't usher in the kingdom of God, nor will it ensure eternal treasures.

Money is a cheap but powerful substitute for Jesus, and wielding money is intoxicating, but it won't usher in the kingdom of God, nor will it ensure eternal treasures.

In my quest for fame and fortune—oh, how it pains me to write it—I forgot to lift my eyes heavenward. I forgot the end of the story. The psalmist warned,

> *So don't be impressed with those who get rich*
> *and pile up fame and fortune.*
> *They can't take it with them;*
> *fame and fortune all get left behind.*
> *Just when they think they've arrived*
> *and folks praise them because they've made good,*
> *They enter the family burial plot*
> *where they'll never see sunshine again.* (Ps. 49:16–17 MSG)

LEARN TO BE PROACTIVE

True, you can't take it with you. But our lives should be more than simply choosing not to grab at money. It's more than plain relinquishment. It must be proactive, where we see everything we've been given as a gift to use to further God's kingdom. Hudson Taylor said, "The less I spent on myself and the more I gave to others, the fuller of happiness and blessing did my soul become."[1] Author Randy Alcorn put it beautifully: "God prospers me not to raise my standard of living, but to raise my standard of giving."[2]

Although I don't see it from my Texas suburb, this world has large pockets of people who live below the poverty line, many who can't find potable water. Many die from preventable diseases, and others suffer under terrible regimes, unable to feed their families because of war-torn chaos. Looking at these folks with such huge problems makes me wonder about the kingdom of God being present here. I could spend a lot of time questioning God about why bad things happen to folks, but that argument becomes fruitless when I realize the simple truth that we are blessed to be a blessing. Our wealth is one means God uses to rescue others. If I hold tightly to what I perceive as mine, instead of understanding that my wealth is something I manage, not own, I will close my eyes and tighten my fist to the needs of this world. And I'll shortchange my growth.

Because true growth happens not in the hoarding but in the releasing. Stagnation comes when we deify the almighty dollar. Solomon had pointed words to say about those who cling to wealth:

> Those who love money will never have enough. How meaningless to think that wealth brings true happiness! The more you have, the more people come to help you spend it. So what good is wealth—except perhaps to watch it slip through your fingers! People who work hard sleep well, whether they eat little or much. But the rich seldom

get a good night's sleep. There is another serious problem I have seen under the sun. Hoarding riches harms the saver. Money is put into risky investments that turn sour, and everything is lost. In the end, there is nothing left to pass on to one's children. We all come to the end of our lives as naked and empty-handed as on the day we were born. We can't take our riches with us. And this, too, is a very serious problem. People leave this world no better off than when they came. All their hard work is for nothing—like working for the wind. Throughout their lives, they live under a cloud—frustrated, discouraged, and angry. (Eccl. 5:10–17 NLT)

Folks married to money think about it constantly, lose sleep, get taken advantage of, spend it all, lose it all, and struggle with futility. Reading that scripture pauses me because at first I read it as an outsider, thinking it has nothing to do with middle-

True growth happens not in the hoarding but in the releasing.

class me. But honestly I live as if I believe Solomon's words, "that wealth brings true happiness." It's a powerful myth that many in this society believe, one the media and entertainment industry tout. Money equals happiness. Yet Jesus says it's better to give away than to receive.

• • •

Thankfully, the latter half of Ecclesiastes 5 offers us hope:

Even so, I have noticed one thing, at least, that is good. It is good for people to eat, drink, and enjoy their work under the sun during the short life God has given them, and to accept their lot in life. And it is a good thing to receive wealth from God and the good health to enjoy it. To enjoy your work and accept your lot in life—this is indeed a gift from God. God keeps such people so busy enjoying life that they take no time to brood over the past. (vv. 18–20 NLT)

God created us to thrive and work, to enjoy what we create. As we grow we learn to accept our lot in life, to enjoy life so much that we forget the past and anticipate the future. If we're tangled in despair or fear over money, we cannot grow. But if we open our hands before the Lord, with a heart full of gratitude and humble acceptance, if we see ourselves as managers of His wealth and rejoice when we're able to give to others, we will grow: "The generous will prosper; those who refresh others will themselves be refreshed" (Prov. 11:25 NLT).

QUESTIONS FOR REFLECTION AND DISCUSSION

- *How much of each day do you spend worrying about money?*

- *Looking back over the past decade, how has God provided for you? How did your faith grow during lean years? Stagnate?*

- *Randy Alcorn wrote, "God prospers me not to raise my standard of living, but to raise my standard of giving." How has your standard of giving risen over the past few years?*

- *Why did Jesus harp so much about money? Why is it tied to our hearts?*

- *How does God want you to relinquish money right now?*

Chapter Fourteen

RECONCILE THE PARADOX OF FAILURE

To dry one's eyes and laugh at a fall,
And, baffled, get up and begin again . . .

—ROBERT BROWNING[1]

I WATCHED THE MAN ON TV FLASH HIS PLASTIC SMILE AND spout empty promises. All I need to do is think happy thoughts, live in the land of positivity, and God will owe me a perfect life. Other preachers tell me it's my right to live trial-free, to have money in the bank and in my pockets, to be immune from pestilence (which has always been a paradox to me. Don't we all die? Are we supposed to be healthy all our lives until the day we suddenly expire with a smile on our faces?).

This view that God is a supercomputer—and all we need to do is to program Him correctly by saying the right commands so He'll give us everything we want—is heretical. But even more insidious is another common belief: that if we obey God, success will be the unavoidable outcome.

But what if we feel empty-handed after a trial? What if we've done everything we can, placing our hands in Jesus', only to wonder why He led us on that journey in the first place? What if serving Him hurts? How do we catalog that kind of failure? Do we give in to despair, believing God doesn't want to prosper us as the TV preachers say?

Or is there another aspect of failure we cannot see? A paradoxical way? A kingdom path?

DOES GOD ALWAYS CALL US TO SUCCESS?

An acquaintance wrote to me after we returned from our time overseas. She wanted to know if we felt we made a mistake by going there in the first place. The implication of her question was that perhaps we missed God's will because we didn't ultimately succeed. Her question reminds me of my solo six-week mission trip to Malaysia after college. Although some cool Jesus things blossomed there, what mostly happened was that I got very sick, ended up in the hospital emergency room, and then grew sicker. I followed Jesus halfway around the world to turn green. Hardly a story of victory. And yet God used that trip to ignite a passion for the world in me.

Or the time I believed God called me to China, so I took the GRE test for graduate school two weeks before my wedding and (surprise!) performed terribly. There would be no English as a Second Language graduate school in my life, at least not at that time. I felt terribly small when the results came back, but God used it to move me in another direction, and the failure kept me humble and teachable.

Or the time I tried to start a Young Life club at the junior high where I taught—a ministry that blossomed, wilted, then died. It could be that I'm a great starter, a terrible finisher, which certainly can be true, but it could also mean that God works brilliantly in failures. Not in outward success, but inwardly. Failure sanctifies, bringing us closer to Him. It may not look like ministry glory, but it becomes soul glory.

Or the weeks, months, and years I poured into high school girls, wondering whether anything I said or prayed or encouraged meant anything in the grand scheme of God's kingdom. At times I sensed God's hand, but most of what He required of me was blind obedience.

In light of those recollections, I wrestled with answering my friend with accuracy and grace and a kingdom perspective. I responded with this:

The question you ask is one I wrestle with. In retrospect, I realize we did what God asked us to do. He didn't promise success; He simply required obedience. And that's where I have to rest. Looking back, we endured hardship upon hardship, far too many to list. But we came through. Wounded and battle weary, yes, but still loving Jesus and able to endure far more than we'd ever been able to before.

Was a church planted? Yes. Was it easy? No. Do we question God? Sometimes. Coming home, do we feel defeat? Absolutely. Why? Because we don't look "successful" by returning after two and a half years.

It's an American idea that if you obey God, blessings will always follow. Success is yours—guaranteed. Your ultimate life awaits you. Striving after success (in terms of the world's standards) in this life is sorely misguided and misplaced. The heroes of the faith obey and pretty terrible things happen to them. I love this verse in Hebrews: "And all these things, having gained approval through their faith, did not receive what was promised, because God has provided something better for us" (Hebrews 11:39–40 NASB). Our ultimate reward awaits us in heaven.

We ventured overseas because we love Jesus, because He asked us to go. In that call to us, He did not say, "Obey and everything will go smoothly. A mega church will be planted. You'll find success at every turn, if only you'd obey me." Actually, it goes more like this:

"Obey. Experience financial, relational, spiritual, familial trials like you've never encountered before. Slog your way through. Love folks who betray. Teach people. Endure. Fall down. Get back up, only to fall again. Pray a lot. And leave the results (which may look dubious) to Me."

The deeper issue is trust. Will we trust Jesus to lead, even when His leading looks like failure? Do we love Him enough to follow Him down that road? Or will we only follow Him where success looms on the horizon like a beckoning sunrise?

I don't worry so much about missing God's highest will, or bumbling a mistake, or going somewhere where He may not lead or He may lead. I try to trust that whatever path He leads me on, that I will lean into the lessons He sends my way. To learn about death and resurrection. To go through trials that crucify my selfishness.

I worry that I'll become narcissistic, where the world revolves around me-me-me. Obeying Jesus is one of the methods He's used to root out my narcissism. Thanks be to God! Yesterday I read this quote: "We must die to ourselves before we are turned into gentleness, and our crucifixion involves suffering. It will mean experiencing genuine brokenness and a crushing of self, which will be used to afflict the heart and conquer the mind."[2] That is the blessing of obedience to me. Brokenness. Crushing of self. Affliction of heart. A conquered mind. I won't trade those lessons for a mountaintop of personal glory any day, though the path to get there is excruciating.

I'm not sure I answered your question, but I sure thank you for asking it. It caused me to reflect and consider. Did we obey? Yes. And the results of that obedience are held sweetly in His hands.

When others have suffered under failure as I have, I send them this e-mail as an encouragement. God is not finished with us. He uses everything in our lives to prepare us for the next wild step. He is bigger than our missteps, thankfully.

THE PARADOXICAL BENEFITS OF SUFFERING AND FAILURE

When we suffer, God crucifies our ambition, burying it deep in the hollow of our ambitious souls. We may not like the pain it takes to be freed from this. We may fight the Almighty because we hunger for success. We enjoy telling victorious stories. But sometimes those stories aren't real. I remember coming back to our Texas church during a particularly trying time overseas, speaking to several Sunday school classes, breaking down during each talk. I sputtered a few words and then cried. One thing I managed to say was a quote I remember from an Urbana missions conference: "When God wants to do an impossible task, He takes an impossible person and breaks her."

A friend found me a few weeks ago and said, "Mary, I wrote down what you said in our Sunday school class years ago and reread it today. That quote still resonates with me."

So the mysterious plan of God continues. He uses failure to break us so we can bless another broken friend, who then will

When we suffer, God crucifies our ambition, burying it deep in the hollow of our ambitious souls.

no doubt touch another in her brokenness. It's the gospel of the broken, inaugurated by Jesus' broken body on the cross, advanced through our weakness.

I think of Paul and his paradoxical life, certainly not chock-full of victories. Yet often we envision a lofty man, engraved in stone, the epitome of strength and valor—a missionary of missionaries. He never failed in missions, right? Yet he enjoyed boasting about his weakness (2 Cor. 12:9–10). What kind of man was he who gladly boasted about his inferiority? What will God have to pull me through to inaugurate that same state of gladness? I may boast in my weaknesses, but gladly? Looking back on my mistakes, I recount much of them in sorrow, not joy. I hope for the day to come when I can point to my failure with a smile, accompanied by a deep knowing that Christ's power evidences itself far more in my failure than my Mary-generated victory.

I am not living in the Paul place yet, where I can boldly boast of my weakness. Not to the place of contentment with a laundry list of

What will God have to pull me through to inaugurate that same state of gladness?

stress and insults. But with even a tiny bit of hindsight, I see beauty in Paul's words. I deal better with insults and persecutions. I handle distresses and difficulties more aptly. I want to come to the place where I realize that obedience involved more about crucifying shreds (and whole garments) of my pride and ego than it did about ministry success or failure.

LEARNING TO DIMINISH

Living the everything life is all about enlarging and diminishing. As John the Baptist said of Jesus, "He must increase, but I must decrease" (John 3:30). Failure is the crucible God uses to increase Jesus and decrease us. It's the venue God uses to increase our capacity for Himself. "For You," the psalmist said, "will enlarge my heart" (Ps. 119:32 NASB). The funny thing is I feel awfully small after failure. But my heart? It's growing.

We may not understand the pathways God lays out before us. We may not even like walking the journey. But even in failure, we can trust that He'll do more than we expect. That's the paradoxical way God brings us closer to Himself, where we stop asking, "Why me?" and instead rest in "Why not me?"

• • •

Growth comes in the aftermath of failure, not wild success. What we do with it matters. How we respond to falling down reveals where we stand today, and what we decide to do right now determines our growth rate for the future. Like Paul, we can experience hardship upon hardship. And if we want to have an impact like Paul, we must choose, once again, to see that hardship as normative in the kingdom of God, dust off ourselves, lean into God's strength, and simply do the next thing He asks of us.

Growth comes in the aftermath of failure, not wild success. What we do with it matters.

Sometimes I wish life were as easy as some of the TV preachers say. Think positive thoughts. Always be victorious and successful. But where would the mystery be? I would hate to follow a knowable, tame God who takes me down mundane, well-traveled paths. In that, we would never know the availability of God's ability.

QUESTIONS FOR REFLECTION AND DISCUSSION

- *In retrospect, how has failure shaped you in a positive way? Negative?*

- *When was the last time failure immobilized you from doing something risky?*

- *Knowing what you do about Jesus' ability to turn failure around, how can you frame your next failure?*

- *Why doesn't God want us continually healthy and wealthy? Why wouldn't He want to give us everything we want, including success?*

- *Who in your life has experienced this chapter, walking through failure and thriving on the other side? How can that story encourage you today?*

Grow Better Together

God's most beautiful jewels are often delivered in rough packages
by very difficult people, but within the package we will find the
very treasures of the king's palace and the Bridegroom's love.

—A. B. Simpson[1]

I persevere through trials pretty well. Throw money issues my way and I'll complain and worry, but inevitably I learn to place that stressor in God's capable grasp. Pull out the rug from underneath my ambitions, and I lick my wounds, reframe my goals, and take the next step. But add relational discord to any pedestrian trial, and I crumble.

The truth in this life: people we trust betray us. Underhanded words assail, penetrate, and disassemble our hearts. In the midst of relentless discouragement, when we have to confront and retreat, our support system fractures. Instead of leaving us alone to regroup, some painful relationships recoil, then shark-bite back.

I sat across from one of those relationships, a woman to whom I'd given my heart. We gathered around a bistro table at a quaint lunch spot, another friend making three. We bantered over our menu selections. Made small talk.

When I first met this woman, I sensed inauthenticity, a beautiful facade covering something painful. So I determined to be a model for her, to practice vulnerability, to parade the joy of honesty and Velveteen Rabbit realness. I must've forgotten the words, "Above all else, guard your heart, for it is the wellspring of life" (Prov. 4:23 NIV). As our friendship deepened, I shared my innermost fears. Over several months, she discovered my worry that I wouldn't be a good mommy, that I constantly thought I never measured up. As a pioneer parent who didn't want to duplicate my childhood home, I lived with a tentacled fear that I would repeat the pain I'd experienced as a child, that I'd parent by neglecting, that I couldn't nurture well or enough. She understood this about me.

The conversation, light and buoyant, flitted to our children as babies, remembering how quickly they grew up. My friend looked me in the eyes, leveling her gaze, then said, "You know, Mary, I can't imagine you ever holding a baby."

Fork midair, my heart stopped a moment. Her words wept into me. My internal accusation seethed. I'd never be a nurturer, a baby holder. My friend recorded every shred of my vulnerability, then waited until the perfect moment to slay me with those words. As I type them now, they feel less burdensome because years of healing fill the space between the utterance and today. Still, they cut.

Never one to respond in the moment to criticism or mean talk, I accepted her words, smiled, and died inside. Later in the shelter of our tiny villa, I processed my hurt with Patrick. There I realized just how much those words broke me. I later shared with her how her words hurt me. She smiled and said that was not what she meant. But her eyes told me a different story. She meant it, and I circled the drain.

I broke because of cancerous community. While I know that those harmed in community must also heal in community, I can't seem to want the remedy to the pain in that way.

WHY COMMUNITY WHEN IT'S SO PAINFUL?

Why does God ask us to risk in relationship again after so much betrayal and heartache? Why would God ask us to delve into the very thing that broke us? Aren't we wise to guard our hearts?

Though I know that the pathway to healing and growth lies at the feet of others, my tendency in the aftermath of pain is to push people away, assigning evil motives. I erect ironclad walls, unscalable by even the tenderest disciple.

But community wooed me despite my walls.

The night we flew home from overseas, heads down, eyes tired, hearts heavy, we drove more than an hour in a borrowed car to find a place we'd never been before. Friends of friends opened up an apartment for us in the corner of a barn on a ranch in the middle of nowhere. We were a keyless people, like wandering Israelites over hot Texas highways. Eventually we spied the tiny barn. Christmas lights decorated a corrugated metal roof that jutted out from the tiny apartment. The owners greeted us there, smiling, with Jesus eyes. We stumbled over the threshold, our brood of five bedraggled wanderers, to a sight I will never forget.

Christmas loomed less than a week away, and I'd worried about how to create a celebration amid such heartache. I had no energy to prepare or think ahead. But before us in the living/dining/kitchen sat a Christmas tree, bejeweled and sparkly. Food lined the pantry. The fridge sat full. Cookies, freshly baked, preened on a plate in the middle of a borrowed dining room table. Beds were made. Christmas music jaunted. This barn-home, where horses nickered and cows stomped impatient feet just beyond the interior walls, became a grace cathedral in that moment.

One small piece of my heart that'd been broken off Velcroed itself back to me. Where cynicism threatened to overtake me, a shard of hope emerged. This beautiful rebuilding of what had shattered happened relationship by relationship, and it started in the corner of a barn where our friends dared to extravagantly bless our family at possibly the lowest point of our lives.

GOD USES COMMUNITY TO HEAL US

That's the power of community to heal and grow us. I used to think that healing from wounds delivered by community came through isolation, pulling away from all relationships. Yet God in His paradoxical requests asks us to heal by walking into the very thing that wounded us. If we've been broken in community, He asks us to trust Him enough to let community (hopefully a healthier one) heal us. That's why those who isolate after hurt become bitter people. Left to themselves, they fester in their anger, nurse it, let it disfigure their souls. It's when they choose to risk again that the rough edges smooth, thanks to others who love well.

> *God in His paradoxical requests asks us to heal by walking into the very thing that wounded us.*

While isolation has the potential to mature us—reading the Bible, praying alone, being still before God—community tests that growth. As I look back over my mountains of growth and compare them to the molehills where I stagnated, community often made the difference. In college where the weight of my past crushed, depressed, and debilitated me, people pulled me from the wreckage. They prayed for me, loved me, listened to my stories of woe, dusted me off, and helped set my feet on a firm road. They became like Aaron and Hur who held up Moses' tired arms while a battle raged (Ex. 17). Victory derived from community.

You may read this chapter with a bit of angst burning inside. You've been hurt by other Christians, possibly even Christian leaders. You've become disillusioned with those who carry the name of Christ like a banner. The last thing you want to do is to risk again. Certainly not be vulnerable and open, laid bare for more deceit and pain. Yet the truth remains: we grow in community's embrace.

IT'S NOT ME + JESUS

In our American viewpoint, we've practically dissected community from Christianity. We see it as the *Me + Jesus Show*, touting our personal relationship with God. Yet God never intended us to grow alone. We spend years reading the Bible through individual lenses, when God intends us to read His Word with the church in mind. Consider a very popular verse: "If we confess our sins, he is faithful and just to forgive us our sins and to cleanse us from all unrighteousness" (1 John 1:9).

When we read that verse, we automatically insert an *I* without knowing it. We read it, "If I confess my sins, he is faithful and just to forgive me my sins and to cleanse me from all unrighteousness." Although it is entirely true that God forgives our sins individually, this verse is actually talking about confessing sins in the context of community. John used the word *we*. And the surrounding verses prove this to be true. We are to confess our sins to each other, to live in the light with each other, to forsake sin alongside each other.

Think about that. Remember a time when you confessed a sin to Jesus and asked for forgiveness. Did He forgive you? Yes. But did you feel the impact of that forgiveness? Perhaps. Now recall a time when you openly confessed a sin to a small group of friends. After the confession, did you feel God's forgiveness? Chances are you did. Because of the power of community, of people coming alongside you and bearing the weight of your confession before a holy God. People who can, in a very real sense, act as Jesus to you.

I struggled with a painful sin throughout high school and into college. In my isolation I convinced myself that I was unforgivable, that God must hate me. It took years to come to the place where I could confess it to a friend. When I did, my head hung low to conceal my reddened face. To my surprise, my friend said, "Oh, Mary, many people have struggled with that. I have too. Jesus forgives you." In that moment (and not before), God healed me of years of tormenting shame. And the hold that sin had over me dissipated. In the light of community, God set me free.

Look at the verses leading up to 1 John 1:9, now reading them with community in mind: "This is the message we have heard from him and proclaim to you, that God is light, and in him is no darkness at all. If we say we have fellowship with him while we walk in darkness, we lie and do not practice the truth. But if we walk in the light, as he is in the light, we have fellowship with one another, and the blood of Jesus his Son cleanses us from all sin. If we say we have no sin, we deceive ourselves, and the truth is not in us" (1 John 1:5–8).

> *We walk in truth not merely for our sake, but for the sake of others in our community who need to know the truth.*

Who are we going to say these things to? Ourselves? No, the implication is that we will share our hearts with others. We live in the light not for us, but so that it will shine before others. We walk in truth not merely for our sake, but for the sake of others in our community who need to know the truth. And if we choose to withhold truth from our community, painting on our everything-is-well facade (oh, how many churches operate in this manner!), we are liars.

NO MORE PLAYACTING

We cannot grow in untruth, in playacting, in filling a role at church. God is not after us to be mannequins of perfection; His desire is for us to be real, honest people daring enough to share our hearts. Because that's where growth flourishes. When I address groups around the country, I'm not a typical speaker. I don't follow a prescribed plan, though there was a time in my career I felt I was supposed to. Now I simply share my story, stark and open and raw, but with an eye toward redemption. And afterward, usually a few people will approach me and say, "I used to feel alone. Now I don't." That's why we live our lives freely

We cannot grow in untruth, in playacting, in filling a role at church.

in front of others. That's why we share our stories. So others won't feel alone. That's why my friend's proclamation to me after I confessed my sin changed the course of my life—because I realized how we're all so similar, so needy for Jesus.

THE DANGER OF AUTONOMY

One of Satan's most powerful ploys is to get you alone, to isolate you. And when he does, he wins a victory. The more we pull away from other believers, the more we lurk toward darkness. Which is why the author of Hebrews warned us not to forsake fellowship: "Let us not neglect our meeting together, as some people do, but encourage one another, especially now that the day of his return is drawing near" (Heb. 10:25 NLT).

Acts 4 illuminates some of the best part of community:

The whole congregation of believers was united as one—one heart, one mind! They didn't even claim ownership of their own possessions. No one said, "That's mine; you can't have it." They shared everything. The apostles gave powerful witness to the resurrection of the Master Jesus, and grace was on all of them. And so it turned out that not a person among them was needy. Those who owned fields or houses sold them and brought the price of the sale to the apostles and made an offering of it. The apostles then distributed it according to each person's need. (vv. 32–35 MSG)

In this birth of the embryonic church, believers, united in the Holy Spirit, helped one another. They talked about Jesus, and grace washed them all. They grew so much in that congregation that their wallets were converted immediately, and they sought to meet other needs. Others noticed, and soon persecution inflamed. As the believers scattered, they created new communities of growth and sacrifice, uniting themselves under the authority of the Holy Spirit, sharing a common enemy: Satan.

In our communities of faith, we need this same submission to the Holy Spirit.

In our communities of faith, we need this same submission to the Holy Spirit. Instead of turning on each other, we need to remember our common enemy, Satan. With these two tenets, we learn to live, grow, act, forgive, offer grace, forbear, hold, bless, and rejoice with others.

THE WAY WE CONNECT

In the circle of healthy community, we grow. But how? What can we do today to connect to other believers? Consider the size of groups we lead/interact with and the degree of life transformation that results.

Number in Group	Type of Group	Your Role
3	Inner circle/closest friends	Mentor
12	Disciples	Discipler
70	Small crowd	Facilitator
120	Congregation	Shepherd
120+	Multitudes	Visionary teacher

Obviously we see Jesus in all these roles. As the Leader of the universe, He chose to spend the bulk of His time in the smallest group with Peter, James, and John. He did day-to-day life with the disciples. He interacted with the crowd that pushed in around Him. And sometimes He interacted in a bigger group in the synagogue. Once in a while He addressed the multitudes. Think about the life change each circle brought. Where He spent most of His time, we see the pillars of the church. As we move toward the multitudes, it's harder to quantify measurable growth. All ways of interaction are important, but not all yield genuine life-transforming growth. I've seen this in my life. I might hear a great speaker, and her words might change my perspective, but true growth happens when I process what I learned with a small group of trusted believers.

Which leads me to the question that pokes at us. Where are we spending our time? How are we investing our energy? And how can we strategically think of ways to pour into the people whom God places in our lives? Ask yourself these questions:

- Do I have a small group where my life is transformed and I'm actively a part of helping others grow?
- Am I teachable? Or do I only want to teach? Have I preferred the roar of the crowd in my ministry to the quiet admonition of my closest friends?
- Are there people in my life (including my children) whom I am teaching/discipling? How am I walking alongside people, sacrificing for them, shouldering their burdens?
- How do I manage my time when it comes to impacting my widest circle of friends? Would these people say I'm confrontable?
- What congregation has God called me to? What am I doing to love that congregation?
- How am I ministering to the multitudes? Since Web 2.0, many

of us have more than 120 people we influence. Do I favor this multitude over my smaller circles? Have I learned to budget my time for this group in a way that reflects Jesus' heart?

BE WISE ABOUT YOUR RELATIONSHIPS

Psalm 90:12 (NLT) instructs, "Teach us to realize the brevity of life so that we may grow in wisdom." Our days on this earth are fleeting. We have a chance to broaden and deepen our impact by examining our lives and seeing how we're spending our time with others. There is an important relational line, though—one to be cautiously aware of. As I mentioned earlier, Scripture advises us to guard our hearts. Jesus instructed us not to throw our pearls (the best, most valuable parts of us) before swine (those who abuse, neglect, or take advantage of). Just because we've been hurt by someone doesn't mean we must heal from that hurt by eagerly reengaging that specific person. God uses healthy community to grow us. Walking back into toxicity only damages and embitters us more. Yes, there are appropriate times to guard our hearts.

Another caveat to this messy thing called community: just because we have issues in our hearts doesn't give us license to share every single thing we're thinking with the person in front of us. In an insatiable need to be noticed in my teens, I over-shared my story for the sake of attention. I practically chased people down with my story. The result? People ran away from me, and the attention I desired dried up.

This harkens back to our need to rely on the Holy Spirit even in the way we choose to share with folks. He gently guides us to talk sometimes and refrain other times. That's the beauty of walking by the Spirit. There's no prescription, no list, no exact way to approach relationship. Relying on our relationship with the Holy Spirit and listening to His prompting help us navigate each friendship. He warns us when we've over-shared. He checks us when we're pulling away. He cautions us when we run headlong into an abusive relationship. As the Author of relationships, He is the wise and loving guide we need to thrive in community.

· · ·

Profound growth happens in the context of community. Yes, just as I experienced with my friend, community can be the most painful thing we endure on earth, but God also uses His flawed followers to heal us from those wounds. Will we allow

Profound growth happens in the context of community.

God to heal us in that manner? Do we truly believe He is big enough to walk us through our next experience with community? The writer of Hebrews encouraged all of us when he wrote,

> God is not unjust. He will not forget how hard you have worked for him and how you have shown your love to him by caring for other believers, as you still do. Our great desire is that you will keep on loving others as long as life lasts, in order to make certain that what you hope for will come true. Then you will not become spiritually dull and indifferent. Instead, you will follow the example of those who are going to inherit God's promises because of their faith and endurance. (Heb. 6:10–12 NLT)

As we care for other believers and allow them to care for us, we assure ourselves that we won't become spiritually dull. Yes, it's a risk. Yes, it's painful at times, but the joy of growth on the other end is worth it and impossible without it.

QUESTIONS FOR REFLECTION
AND DISCUSSION

- *When have you pulled away from community? Why? How has God wooed you back in?*

- *Why does God choose to heal us by using the very thing that hurt us?*

- *Would other people examining your life say you enjoy spending time with other believers? How would they see you spending your free time?*

- *Do you actively seek ways to encourage those around you?*

- *Are your conversations bent more toward trying to prove your point or asking great questions so you understand those you interact with?*

Chapter Sixteen

FOLLOW THE LEADER

"Come, follow me," Jesus said.

—MATTHEW 4:19 NIV

TRAILING AFTER OTHERS IS NOT IN MY NATURE. IF YOU see me walk with anyone, my family included, I lead the way. I could argue my legs are long and enjoy a fast pace, but the reality is I like to be in the lead. I like to know that no one impedes my progress, that I will successfully arrive at my destination. It's a bit cracked, I know.

But we are called to be followers of Jesus Christ. Our hands must busy themselves with His tasks, His initiation, not our own. We are called to walk behind Him, letting Him lead us wherever He pleases.

Oddly I like to follow other people's rules or even my own. It's easier for me to look at delineated tasks on a page, make my way through them, than slow down enough to listen to God's directives—to follow His counterintuitive ways. I crave the safety of multiple lists. I like machinations of tasks more than following Jesus. Which can be problematic because as I've studied the New Testament, I've realized something painful: mature believers have fewer rules and more relationship with God. Immature believers are just the opposite. The mark of the weaker brother or sister is an adherence to spiritual lists. Paul battled against that when he wrote to the Colossians:

> You have died with Christ, and he has set you free from the spiritual powers of this world. So why do you keep on following the rules of the world, such as, "Don't handle! Don't taste! Don't touch!"? Such rules are mere human teachings about things that deteriorate as we use them. These rules may seem wise because they require strong devotion, pious self-denial, and severe bodily discipline. But they provide no help in conquering a person's evil desires. (Col. 2:20–23 NLT)

I may think, naively, that I can conquer my evil desires by trying harder and making more rules for myself, but I will miss the beauty and risk of following after the person of Jesus Christ if I do.

What Pharisees Did

What scares me even more is looking at how a law-abiding Pharisee lived. Read through this list. A good Pharisee

- knows scripture, memorizing large portions.
- is an avid, dedicated synagogue member.
- is involved in leadership.
- teaches others.
- gives money.
- obeys biblical rule.
- prays.
- dresses the part.

Aren't these characteristics of good church members? Dutiful Christians? Note that all of these things are external. They are check-off-able. But they don't touch on the heart of a follower. Jesus said this to the Pharisees (oh, how He says this to me): "You search the Scriptures because you think they give you eternal life. But the Scriptures point to me! Yet you refuse to come to me to receive this life" (John 5:39–40 NLT). The Pharisees refused to follow. They adhered to religious tradition, tradition that was meant to point them to Jesus, but they missed Him.

Perhaps this is why so many of us don't truly follow Jesus. George Barna laments this when he writes, "If God provides us with a plan (in scripture) and the power (through the Holy Spirit) to become a full transformed person, why then is it that more than 80 out of 100 Americans call themselves Christian, yet only 1 out of every 100 are broken, surrendered, submitted and loving?"[1]

Consider these statistics according to a recent Barna study:

- Only one of seven believers in Jesus reports that his or her highest priority in life is Jesus.
- Less than one in five Christians is strongly committed to personal growth.
- One in five Christ followers believes becoming a Christian was the most important decision he or she made in life.
- Twenty-two percent of Christians say they believe they're living dependent on God.[2]

WHAT DOES IT MEAN TO FOLLOW?

Jesus calls for nothing less than abandoned following. But what exactly does that look like in the real world? With real people? Who have real problems? Jesus beckons us not to a program, not to do stuff for the sake of being radical, but to Himself. Yes, He's scary. Yes, He's untamed. Yes, He's

Yes, He's scary. Yes, He's untamed. Yes, He's more interested in heart than rule.

more interested in heart than rule. But we have that choice to follow Him every single day. Or fall back into rules, running the Christian show in our own strength.

Think Rightly About God

My husband, Patrick, and I had a long conversation about spiritual growth. We agreed on the importance of following Jesus, not a set of rules. But as we talked, he emphasized two additional tenets in terms of following: right belief and willful action. Patrick said, "It has to be both head and hands. We must think correctly about God, and then obey." Obedience flows after our right beliefs. A. W. Tozer said, "What comes into our minds when we think about God is the most important thing about us."[3] Before we can put walking shoes to our faith, we must think rightly about God. So many of us (me included) construct God in our fallible and meager minds. Because of our finiteness and propensity for sin, we cannot conceive adequately of a God so big, so holy. We remain small-minded believers in a manageable God. We are guilty of reversal—we call the shots, He obeys.

Our actions—what we do with our hands—then flow out of a titanic theology of God—that He is big and we are not. That He is all things wise and we are needy of that wisdom. That He is beyond our comprehension, yet stoops to come to our aid. He is God. We are not. He knows better, so we should follow, not resorting to lists and outward appearance, but appealing to Him so that He will change and move and heal us from the inside out.

Act Right

So, if we believe that God is big, that He is beyond comprehension, how now shall we follow? How will good theology meet the low roads of everyday life?

Step by blessed step.

In that daily struggle, we should shy away from becoming a Barna statistic, turning a deaf ear to Jesus' whispers. We must want Jesus to be the priority and highlight of our lives. We should long to be known as people committed to spiritual growth. In that, we will want people to see our lives and take note of our reliance on Jesus, that we fully depend on Him for everything. That if He were taken from us, we'd lack vibrance and joy.

Me? I want to grow, tall and strong. I want to reach my arms to the heavens and shout Hallelujah! I want my life to emanate Christ in every way, in every relationship, in every decision. In order to do that, I need to know God's enormity as He stoops to meet my inability. In my frailty, I am strong. In my small willingness to walk the paths He has for me, He meets me, enabling me to live as a disciple who thinks right thoughts about God and who walks out those beliefs here on *terra firma*.

After emphasizing right belief, Patrick said that the reason so many Christians live anemic lives, seemingly devoid of power and growth, is that we fail to act. (Before I continue, let me assure you that I have often slid into this area, preferring lethargy to movement.) Growth in the Christian life, he said, lies more in what we do with our belief than merely our statement of it. This is the hands of our belief. We can say we believe Jesus until our faces turn blue. We can try to prove our piety by observing churchy rules and being good people. But we will not demonstrate growth until we make a choice to live out our belief on the pavement of real life.

Jesus made a terribly haunting comment when He asked His disciples, "Why do you keep calling me 'Lord, Lord!' when you don't do what I say?" (Luke 6:46 NLT). Following means taking action. It means slowing down our pace of life enough to actually hear what Jesus is saying, then choosing to do exactly what He says. Otherwise our calling Him *Lord* becomes a farce. James told us that faith without works is dead (James 2:17). Growth happens in the context of movement, of forward momentum where we choose to exercise what we believe.

In practical terms, this means that a new Christian can grow feet to our inches simply because he's acting out his newfound belief in God. Without belief-fueled action, there is atrophy. And without the heart of Christ in the center of our actions, we cannot sustain our growth.

> *Without the heart of Christ in the center of our actions, we cannot sustain our growth.*

The question becomes: Do we really believe God is big enough to take care of us if we dare to follow Him? Truly? If so, why haven't we stepped out into the unknown, where He beckons? If we continually walk away from His directives and gentle encouragements, we will deafen to His whispers and quit growing spiritually. We can stretch and grow in knowledge, but if that does not result in a practical walking out of an inner belief, then we'll stagnate. We may sound smart, profound even, but if we don't step the belief to the pavement of this world, our walk with Jesus will seldom progress beyond today's commonplace spiritual anemia.

PAINLESS CHRISTIANITY

Though we may say we want to grow, many of us also want a painless Christianity. A convenient one. Which is why we bend toward lists, gravitating toward messages about our best lives, seven steps to a meaningful you, how to find daily victory. We equate the benefits of living in our culture (fame, status, a comfortable life) with Christianity. I'm not saying we can't live blessed lives if we follow Jesus. But we often neglect the hard places of obedience in favor of the blessings only.

David Platt put it this way: "We have unnecessarily (and unbiblically) drawn a line of distinction, assigning the obligations of Christianity to a few while keeping the privileges of Christianity for us all."[4] We can't have both. To follow Jesus means to do what He asks of us, and sometimes He asks us to let go of fame, give away our things, and choose discomfort. The growth we experience when we do that is the blessing. Unfortunately we've mistaken the trinkets of ease for the blessings of the kingdom.

In our bent toward instant gratification, we need to be aware that spiritual growth happens over a lifetime. The sanctification journey toward living an Everything life is a process initiated when we first meet Jesus and continues until the day we see Him face-to-face. We may not see measurable growth day by day, but taken in light of eternity, our growth is significant and measured. Because God initiates growth, observes it, and creates it.

We've mistaken the trinkets of ease for the blessings of the kingdom.

JUST FOLLOW

Jesus initiated the disciples' sanctification journey by asking them to leave their livelihood. In a word, He said, "Follow." In that moment, He established His lordship over the disciples' lives and their long-term growth. Where He walked, they walked. Where He preached, they listened. Where He fed, they ate. Their livelihoods rested in His capable hands. Their journey, from the outside, appeared chaotic, but Jesus assured them that He watched His Father work, then followed His instructions exactly. Which is what we are called to do. Watch Jesus, then follow His words. He said, "If you try to hang on to your life, you will lose it. But if you give up your life for my sake, you will save it" (Luke 9:24 NLT).

To follow is to give up our lives, particularly our expectations of how our lives should be. We need to let go of our presumptions about the life we should have and let Jesus dream a new dream for us. A dream where others are changed through the Holy Spirit in us. A dream we can't even fathom. We shortchange ourselves when we delegate our Christianity to a compartment of our lives, managing it on the side, doing Christian things, going through the motions. We miss the mystery, the daring adventure, the growth. Remember this truth: "No eye has seen, no ear has heard, and no mind has imagined what God has prepared for those who love him" (1 Cor. 2:9 NLT).

BECOME THE ANSWER TO SOMEONE'S PRAYER

Oswald Chambers lived such a life. After wrestling with himself and his tendency toward personal perfection and finding that pursuit empty, he chose to lay down his life for Jesus, committing to become a follower of Him. This led him and his wife on missional adventures around the world. In a letter dated February 16, 1907, Oswald Chambers wrote,

> I want to tell you a growing conviction with me, and that is that as we obey the leading of the Spirit of God, we enable God to answer the prayers of other people. I mean that our lives, my life, is the answer to someone's prayer, prayed perhaps centuries ago. It is more and more impossible to me to have programs and plans because God alone has the plan, and our plans are only apt to hinder Him, and make it necessary for Him to break them up. I have the unspeakable knowledge that my life is the answer to prayers, and that God is blessing me and making me a blessing entirely of His sovereign grace and nothing to do with my merits, saving as I am bold enough to trust His leading and not the dictates of my own wisdom and common sense.[5]

People who ardently follow Jesus Christ find themselves in that same happy place. It's good and right to obey the Spirit of God's leadings, but it's even more compelling to think that as we obey those promptings, we become an answer to a prayer, whether that prayer be uttered yesterday or a thousand yesterdays. Doesn't that shake you to the core? And doesn't that realization give you a holy excitement to follow Jesus, even in what seems silly? It makes me want to live today in anticipation of what the Spirit may say to me. To abandon my agenda for His. To spend myself.

Yet I struggle. I'm a program girl. A list maker. One who loves control and order. So many times, I'm afraid. My need to control my environment and feel safe becomes the very idol that dethrones God. My plans "are only apt to hinder Him, and make it necessary for Him to break them up." Oh, but I cling. I believe, falsely, that I can usher peace, security, and hope into my life through skillful manipulation of my schedule and personal rules. But schedules and rules don't save me. They enslave me to myself.

FAITH IN GOD'S FAITHFULNESS

I grew up believing that I was my sole protector, that if I were to be taken care of, I'd have to be the chief safety officer. This led to protection, yes, but it also led to an insatiable need for control, which doesn't bode well for following. God wants to interrupt my plans. Sometimes He wants to messy my life. Always He wants my first allegiance—not allegiance to my personal protection, but allegiance to trust Him first and foremost.

Chambers was a contemporary of Hudson Taylor. At one gathering, Chambers heard Taylor speak. He wrote, "Hudson Taylor said last night that Our Lord's words 'Have faith in God' really mean 'Have faith in the faithfulness of God,' not in your own faithfulness."[6] We often have faith in our own faithfulness. Or trust in our sole ability to provide. And when things go south and we fret about the future, we may spend too much time scheming how to extricate ourselves from our situation. No. We must instead have faith in the faithfulness of God. To let go of worry and follow God's plans. To regard His ways and methods as superior to ours, even if they appear risky or frivolous or foolish.

• • •

The Pharisees missed God in the flesh standing before them. They loved rules over relationship. They couldn't follow what they couldn't control. They refused to follow what couldn't translate into a checklist. Instead of holding a high view of God, they had such a view of themselves, preferring to follow their own paths. They became their own everythings. They appeared to be religious and terrific church members, yet their hearts were far from Jesus, and their actions indicated their distance. I don't want to be them. I want to follow Jesus, to trust that He has the whole wide world in His scarred, beautiful hands. He who died on my behalf and yours deserves our unswerving obedience, our actions, our hearts.

QUESTIONS FOR REFLECTION AND DISCUSSION

- *Why is it important to think rightly about God?*

- *What has tripped you up in the way you follow Jesus this year? Has it been hard to follow Him? Easy? Why?*

- *What practical things has Jesus asked you to do in the last month? How have you taken action? Why or why not?*

- *What is your biggest fear in truly abandoning your agenda for God's?*

- *How does knowing spiritual growth happens over a lifetime encourage you? How does it stress you out? Looking back over your life, what times have you grown the most? Why?*

BECOME IRRESISTIBLE

*Simon Peter answered him, "Lord, to whom shall
we go? You have the words of eternal life."*

—JOHN 6:68

DECADES AGO I DISCOVERED THAT I WASN'T REALLY A
Christian. I'd been walking with Jesus several years and loved Him
deeply, but I apparently didn't love Him enough. In my circle of
Christian friends, I learned that listening to the 1980s boy band Duran
Duran bordered on blasphemy. "That music doesn't honor Jesus," one
friend said. "You should only listen to Christian music."

I wavered back and forth between berating myself for listening to
Satan's music and really liking the bands he apparently inspired. But
the social pressure was so strong to conform that I felt like if I didn't
destroy my music, Jesus wouldn't like me anymore and I'd be cut off
from His favor on my life. So I threw all my pagan music away. I broke
my records in half and threw them down the garbage chute. And felt
better about it for a time. But now I know following Jesus has little to
do with the music I listen to or throw away. It has to do with Jesus, how
He loves me and you and this great big world.

How Do You View the Gospel?

The way in which we view the gospel, the greatest news this world will ever know, is the way in which we will share it. If we view it as the appropriate checklist where our particular view on theology is the only one worth knowing, we will spend our lives trying to coerce people to come to our way of thinking. We'll view others as future converts, not people who are valued and valuable. We are not saved to a checklist of acceptable behaviors. We are saved by an irresistible Savior, one who deserves our allegiance, our lives, and our hearts. He is the wooing God, not a manipulative, coercive deity.

Several years ago, my husband and I met Alan Hirsch and his wife, Deb, church planters in Australia. Alan has also written a lot of books about the church. They spoke to fellow European church plant-ers about this idea of irresistibility. Alan talked about bounded set and centered set theories. Bounded set theory, in terms of church, defines who is out or in, depending on a series of agreed upon beliefs. Picture a fence around a group of people. Those within the fence are "in" because they adhere to the set of beliefs within the square. Those who are "out" are viewed as outsiders. He explained herding practices in the Australian outback where one way to contain your sheep is to build a fence.

When we operate by considering Jesus as the well, drawing all to Himself, we can rest instead in His genuine irresistibility and His ability to draw others to Himself.

It makes perfect sense to me. Those who believe correctly are in. Those who don't are out. And of course, sheep need to be contained, right? Otherwise they'll wander around and find themselves in trouble.

He continued by presenting the centered set theory: people are defined not by whether they're in or out, but by whether they walk a journey toward the center or away from it. "Picture Jesus as the center," he said. In this model, folks are neither in nor out, insiders nor outsiders. They're all viewed as living a journey, moving away from God or toward Him. Then he told us about how most farmers keep sheep nearby in Australia. "They dig a well," he said, "and the sheep naturally stay near."

I have some trouble with the model since I believe there are absolutes. Jesus does say some important things, like the way to Him is a narrow one and few are those who find it, and if we're not for Him, we're against Him. But the fence and the well forever changed the way I view Jesus, His world, and the way I live and share Him. When we operate with a fence mentality, we constantly define who is in and out by our personal theological construct. But when we operate by considering Jesus as the well, drawing all to Himself, we can rest instead in His genuine irresistibility and His ability to draw others to Himself.

THE POWER OF IRRESISTIBILITY

How does this tie in to becoming more like Jesus? If we believe in an irresistible Savior and we are to be His followers, we can measure our growth by how much we are like Him. How, exactly, am I demonstrating Jesus' irresistibleness? How does my life woo people toward Him? How am I like a well, drawing people? And if I'm not, why? Do I rely more on rules and regulations than on my relationship with an irresistible Savior?

This breeds a tender view of people that I often lack. We see the irresistibility of Jesus as He touched people when He walked the earth. Crowds couldn't get enough of Him. And while it is true that many followed Him out of selfish desire (I want to be healed; I want to be important; I want to be near all that power), many followed Him because He held them spellbound by His words and actions. He spoke the words of God, then backed up those words with extreme, yet consistent action.

He loved the outcast and the outsider. And those on the fringes repaid Him with lavish devotion, washing His feet with hair and expensive perfume, following Him even when it meant death, inviting Him to homes for feasts, leaving fishing nets for the sake of fishing for people. Jesus and His passion for the people He created inspired great devotion. Oh, how He loved them!

If we are to be irresistible like Him, we must love as He did, which means having our eyes reopened to the needs of the outcasts of this world—the poor, the lonely, the imprisoned, the needy, the hurting. We don't have to venture far to find those folks, even in the United States. As a wealthy nation, we are just as poverty stricken in our souls, only we've found ways to cover up our sicknesses with appearance, money, walls, and denial. Mother Teresa said it well, "The most terrible poverty is loneliness, and the feeling of being unloved."[1] To be like Jesus is to find the lonely and unloved and take them by the hand not to a fenced-in pasture, but to the well, Jesus.

BECOMING INTERRUPTIBLE

In light of that, our lives become interruptible. We no longer see people as stepping-stones or as obstacles but as folks well loved by Jesus. And He often brings those people in our lives to challenge us, to take our eyes off our capability and look instead on His ability to transform others. And in the process, we are transformed.

I had the opportunity recently to listen to a friend who walked through some painful things. I wanted to turn away, to disengage, but the Holy Spirit within me prompted otherwise. I'm so thankful I stayed, listened, then offered to pray. I watched the burden lift from my friend's shoulders—a holy privilege. Dietrich Bonhoeffer in his groundbreaking community book *Life Together* elaborated, "We must be ready to allow ourselves to be interrupted by God. God will be constantly crossing our paths and canceling our plans by sending us people with claims and petitions. . . . It is part of the discipline of humility that we must not spare our hand where it can perform a service and that we do not assume that our schedule is our own to manage, but allow it to be arranged by God."[2]

I read Bonhoeffer's words and type *amen*. I hope my heart and obedience say amen as well. Our irresistible Savior beckons us toward selflessness, toward becoming irresistible ourselves. We woo others more when we live interruptible lives.

I've marveled lately at how uninterruptible I've been. In some ways, I've missed out on building into people's lives, preferring my work to the messiness of everyday life and relationships. Yet Jesus calls us to be wells, places of refreshment, rest stops for others, even those who differ from us.

UNDERSTAND INSTEAD

One of the most surprising things happened to me while in France. Around the dinner table, for hours at a time, we argued with our French friends. They argued with us and with one another. And then we loved one another, kissed each cheek, and went along our ways. At first it really bothered me. How dare my friends question my politics in such a vehement manner? How could they be so direct and yet, in the aftermath of the conversation, sidle up next to me, kiss both cheeks, and joyfully continue being my friend? That's when I realized that Americans argue differently. The French tend to argue to understand, to share a part of themselves, to put things out on the table, to stimulate a lively discussion. Sometimes they'd play devil's advocate just to stir the pot. I'm not saying this is right or wrong, just different.

Here when folk argue, there has to be a "right" person. In order for that person to be "right," he or she has to decimate the other person's opinion. There's inherent fear behind everything. If I'm not "right," then something about me must be wrong. Therefore I must find blame in the other person's way of looking at things so I can feel secure. I've been this way. I've been so deeply insecure about my opinions that I felt I needed to undermine others' opinions just to feel okay. I hope that I'm growing. I hope that I'm seeing life as far too complex and opinions too multilayered to have such a black-and-white perspective. And through all that, I think again about Jesus and His irresistibility.

We see Jesus hanging out with people who had vastly different life-styles than what was considered "holy" in His day. Tax collectors and sinners flocked to Him. He seemed to invite them near. Children ran to His irresistibility. He was unafraid of others' opinions. He always spoke the truth seasoned with grace. He kept His harshest, most pointed words for those who appeared religious but were hypocritical, while He maintained an invitational stance to the masses. So much so that thousands of people followed Him.

WHAT ABOUT POLITICAL DISCUSSIONS?

My question: Do we represent the irresistibility of Jesus when we discuss politics with someone from the "other side"? Would Jesus yell at someone who differed in her political opinion? Would He lash out? Would He scream? Do shouting and pouting and stirring up fear represent Jesus' manner of doing things? Consider this wisdom from Proverbs, remembering that Jesus is Wisdom personified: "An arrogant man stirs up strife, but he who trusts in the LORD will prosper" (28:25 NASB); and "A fool always loses his temper, but a wise man holds it back" (29:11 NASB). And then from the book of James: "This you know, my beloved brethren. But everyone must be quick to hear, slow to speak and slow to anger; for the anger of man does not achieve the righteousness of God" (1:19–20 NASB).

> *Do shouting and pouting and stirring up fear represent Jesus' manner of doing things?*

We are more winsome when we listen. When we hold back our temper, when we choose not to stir up strife for the sake of proving our "correctness." Our job is not to convince others of their wrongness and our rightness. It's not to change people's hearts. (We did not create anyone's heart as far as I know. Only God can change a heart.) Our job is to represent Jesus, how He talked, how He acted, how He loved, how He wooed. We should be so settled in His love for us that very little threatens us. Very little shakes us up. We know how to entrust ourselves to God. We know how to wrestle. We know how to trust.

How Well Do We Love Those Who Differ?

The litmus test is this: How well do we love those who differ from us? I'd venture to say that God will not hold us accountable for our political bent or fervor as much as He'll call us to account for the way we love those who hold a different view. We are to be as Jesus was (and is and is to come): irresistible sources of life. Do others flock to us for sustenance? Or do they back away from us because we've created impenetrable boundaries around us? What would it look like if we viewed everyone as a fellow pilgrim on a difficult, earthly journey? What if we loved them enough to welcome discord and different opinions?

The litmus test is this: How well do we love those who differ from us?

Why is this important? Because we never grow in a vacuum, away from people. We grow when we risk in relationships. But if we love only those who love us or agree with us, we'll never have the opportunity to exercise irresistible love! We spend, I fear, more time accumulating people around us who are yes-folk, who nod joyfully at our correct opinions, forgetting that much is to be learned by interacting with those who differ. We cannot be sharpened or honed by conformity.

Our tendency is to wall off, define our boundaries, and exclude people who don't fit our expectations. Yet Jesus obliterated that fence when the temple veil ripped in two from top to bottom. He opened up the possibility for relationship because of His death on the cross. He gave us access not only to Himself but also to the world He so wildly loved. Because He is the great Reconciler, we can lay ourselves low before the cross and ask His help. Empowered by His Spirit within us, we can love those who differ, grow like crazy, and become irresistible Jesus followers.

Jesus Is the Well

On a blustery day, the clouds dropped wheelbarrows full of water on the streets. Yet I noticed sprinklers turned on, watering where water puddled. We cannot be our own storm. We are not our own well. We may try irrigation, but when the rain pours, it's best to realize it's silly to keep trying to water on our own. Jesus is our Living Water source, but often we rely on anything and everything else to satisfy our thirst. Jeremiah warned us about our penchant for creating our own source:

> *My people have done two evil things:*
> *They have abandoned me—*
>   *the fountain of living water.*
> *And they have dug for themselves cracked cisterns*
>   *that can hold no water at all!* (Jer. 2:13 NLT)

Watering our lawns while the rain pours is not only as futile as digging our own broken cistern (a place for stagnant, not living, water), it's dismissing the ultimate source of water. In our quest to be irresistible, growing followers of Jesus, we must remember that He is the irresistible One. And by His refreshment, we become His irresistible followers.

• • •

We don't become irresistible followers by following the rules. Those expectations—the ones others place on us, the ones we expect for others—don't save us or even better us. Jesus does all that as organically as a rainstorm over thirsty land. I'd like to think Jesus laughed a bit when I single-handedly destroyed my evil music. I picture Him dancing to Duran Duran in the midst of a crowd of others, laughing, cajoling, enjoying life in the moment. His laughter is the beat that beckons Democrats, Republicans, atheists, lesbians, anarchists, farmers, widows, strugglers, addicts, the religiously pious, and even the likes of me toward Him. He's that irresistible.

QUESTIONS FOR REFLECTION AND DISCUSSION

- *How do the bounded set and the centered set change the way you view Jesus, the church, and people in the world?*

- *In what ways is Jesus irresistible to you?*

- *Who do you know who exemplifies the irresistibility of Jesus?*

- *How well do you love those who differ politically from you? Do you tend to see people with different opinions as villains? Why or why not?*

- *Has there been a Duran Duran moment in your life? Where you were told to behave a certain way to be more of a Christian? What happened?*

Chapter Eighteen

Walk Out Surprising Disciplines

> *Don't you realize that in a race everyone runs, but only one*
> *person gets the prize? So run to win! All athletes are disciplined*
> *in their training. They do it to win a prize that will fade away,*
> *but we do it for an eternal prize. So I run with purpose in every*
> *step. I am not just shadowboxing. I discipline my body like an*
> *athlete, training it to do what it should. Otherwise, I fear that*
> *after preaching to others I myself might be disqualified.*
>
> —1 Corinthians 9:24–27 nlt

Today I participated in an exercise boot camp where my instructor systematically tried to kill me. Thankfully I survived. She asked us to take a lap around our park, to speed walk the first, then run the second (mine was more a jog). I've lagged behind all the muscled ladies in my class for several weeks now, but today I outwalked and outran them. I felt invincible, particularly when my instructor noticed. Later in the hour, when my muscles yelled at me, she asked us to take another lap. I finished dead last. All that internal boasting melted into self-pity. It reminded me a lot of this growth journey.

We live in a culture of comparison. We tend to measure our growth not against ourselves but against those folks around us. We see a champion of the faith and feel small. We see a struggling pilgrim, and we amplify ourselves. We forget that growth is a dynamic relationship between us and our Savior. Sure, we need other people as we grow, and God uses others in our journey toward Him, but others can't make us grow. We have to cooperate with the Holy Spirit in our lives if we want to thrive. Simply put, the grass isn't greener on your friend's property; it's greener where you water it.

The grass isn't greener on your friend's property; it's greener where you water it.

Which brings us to the discussion of disciplines—those tasks we do that water our spiritual lives. Our daily decisions to follow Jesus and the fellowship we experience with Him when we truly live on that outer edge of obedience will deeply, profoundly fill and inspire us. So read this chapter against that energized backdrop, with Living Water filling and overflowing us. He gives us the power to dirty our hands in this world.

Although you may have read many good books on spiritual disciplines, I want to shift you off kilter a bit with some unconventional disciplines. These are ten things I've neglected, then discovered, then found great growth in their aftermath.

1. The Discipline of Small Obedience over the Long Haul

Some of the wisest, most spiritually infectious people I've met have grown not simply because of biblical knowledge, but because they dared to obey. Here in the States, with radio and podcasts aplenty keeping us theologically sound, we exegete the life out of Scripture. Blogs, papers, books, sermons all attempt to keep us on the straight and narrow. I'm not disparaging any of that. I'm married to a theologian who thinks deeply about Scripture and feels closest to God when he's wrangling the Bible. Thinking correctly about God is essential. But there's more to growth than knowledge. The Pharisees had bucketloads of knowledge, but they missed understanding Jesus. God in the flesh stood before them, and they dismissed Him. Why? Because they didn't understand the importance of obedience and how it correlated to spiritual understanding.

Growth comes from undecorated obedience.

Growth comes from undecorated obedience. We can study and ponder (and these are worthy exercises), but we really learn the deeper truths of God perched on the precipice of risk, when we dare to jump off into the great unknown of obedience. In that frightening place, we learn His availability, His provision, His guidance much more than if we merely read about His exploits. That's why Christianity should be experiential. The more we dare to obey, the more we experience God. Think of it this way: we have a paint can full of a peaceful blue, but we will not experience its peace if we keep the paint in the can. We must apply it to our bedroom walls first.

I worry about the church's insulation from risk. I read a book once implying that many Christians live as Christian Buddhists. We strive to be free of pain. We do everything to eliminate it. We shy away from risk, from anything seeping of tragedy or difficulty. And yet that's where the treasure lies.

To discern where you are today, ask yourself:

- What does God want me to do today?
- What is He whispering to my heart?
- Am I standing on the precipice of risk, dancing on the edge but never jumping off?

You'll never know depths of spiritual truth if you are unwilling to take the leap. As the hymn goes, we must trust and obey. There's no other way.

2. THE DISCIPLINE OF LETTING HEAVEN BE OUR HEAVEN

If you examine our modern lives, we live better than royalty did in the 1800s and earlier. Indoor plumbing. Heating and air-conditioning. Safe food. Shelter. Health care. Financial security. Heaven is our now. We have everything we need, and in that, we have no need of Jesus. If my friend Paul in Ghana gets sick, he runs to Jesus for help because he cannot afford to see a doctor. My first instinct when my kids are sick is (logically) to take them to the doctor. It's not to pray, I'm sad to say. Because of our affluence, we've edged God right out of our lives.

And yet we do suffer on this earth. Those who suffer understand well the truth that there will be a new heaven and a new earth where wrongs will be righted and tears will be brushed away and hurt will cease its pain. When we dare to live for That Day, our suffering here takes on eternal significance. Frederick William Robertson wrote, "Human nature seems to need suffering to make it fit to be a blessing to the world."[1] When we suffer, we become effective here and bear fruit for the next life. Suffering also enlarges us so earth's clothes no longer fit, so we long to be clothed with Him.

The apostle Paul told us several times that we should be wearing Jesus clothes: "Clothe yourself with the presence of the Lord Jesus Christ. And don't let yourself think about ways to indulge your evil desires" (Rom. 13:14 NLT); and "All who have been united with Christ in baptism have put on Christ, like putting on new clothes" (Gal. 3:27 NLT). These new clothes represent our longing for a different land, where Jesus reigns in His kingdom. We live in that tension between the now and the not yet.

Paul again beckoned us to a different life, a different reality. He lifted our eyes from the dazzle of this world and encouraged us to gaze toward the unseen things: "That is why we never give up. Though our bodies are dying, our spirits are being renewed every day. For our present troubles are small and won't last very long. Yet they produce for us a glory that vastly outweighs them and will last forever! So we don't look at the troubles we can see now; rather, we fix our gaze on things that cannot be seen. For the things we see now will soon be gone, but the things we cannot see will last forever" (2 Cor. 4:16–18 NLT).

When we live for what we cannot see, we grow. When we spend our lives for what we can see, we shrink.[2]

> Anyone who builds on that foundation may use a variety of materials—gold, silver, jewels, wood, hay, or straw. But on the judgment day, fire will reveal what kind of work each builder has done. The fire will show if a person's work has any value. If the work survives, that builder will receive a reward. But if the work is burned up, the builder will suffer great loss. The builder will be saved, but like someone barely escaping through a wall of flames. (1 Cor. 3:12–15 NLT)

I've often feared when I read those verses. I worried that after I died I would see this giant bonfire of my life, where God's holy fire consumed my Mary-centric works, leaving only a tiny shard of silver at its bottom, resting in the ashes of my fear. I don't want to just get by. I don't want to live as if the here and now is everything. The discipline of eternal thinking is a weighty one, but one that must be wrangled. Why? Because this life is our testing ground. It's our training for eternity. How well we obey and love and bless here reflect our reward later.

When we live for what we cannot see, we grow.

When we decide to let heaven be our heaven, we joyfully anticipate this scene: "After this I saw a vast crowd, too great to count, from every nation and tribe and people and language, standing in front of the throne and before the Lamb. They were clothed in white robes and held palm branches in their hands. And they were shouting with a great roar, 'Salvation comes from our God who sits on the throne and from the Lamb!'" (Rev. 7:9–10 NLT). The more we cherish Jesus here and seek His kingdom on this earth, the sweeter our reunion with Him will be. We will have little regret when we see the vast crowds of other believers worshipping the Lamb with abandon.

3. THE DISCIPLINE OF SECRET

Others see so much of what we do, yet God often rewards us in secret. In secret, we lay ourselves bare before our Creator. God does not always call us to live out loud; sometimes He calls us to the quiet and the secret. In the discipline of secret, where we keep some things quiet and bless others behind the scenes, we rest, knowing that even if another person doesn't see us, God does. He instructs us to give and pray in secret:

> When you give to the needy, do not let your left hand know what your right hand is doing, so that your giving may be in secret. And your Father who sees in secret will reward you. And when you pray, you must not be like the hypocrites. For they love to stand and pray in the synagogues and at the street corners, that they may be seen by others. Truly, I say to you, they have received their reward. But when you pray, go into your room and shut the door and pray to your Father who is in secret. And your Father who sees in secret will reward you. (Matt. 6:3–6)

God reciprocates too. He entrusts His secrets to us when we revere Him (Ps. 25:14). Because He calls us and loves us, He gives us secret riches:

I will give you treasures hidden in the darkness—
  secret riches.
I will do this so you may know that I am the LORD,
  the God of Israel, the one who calls you by name. (Isa. 45:3 NLT)

If people hurtle hurtful words our way, He takes us to a secret place and shelters us (Ps. 31:20). When life feels unbearable, He conceals us in His perfect hideaways:

In the day of trouble He will conceal me in His tabernacle;
In the secret place of His tent He will hide me;
He will lift me up on a rock. (Ps. 27:5 NASB)

We serve a God who knows our secrets, shelters us, and discloses His secrets. Often when I'm speaking, God uses my seemingly throw-away phrases to touch others. People will approach me afterward. I expect them to remark about one of my out-there stories, but often they tell me of a forgotten sentence I'd said in passing that blessed them. I receive e-mails from readers touting words I barely remember writing, forgetting the ones I felt were important. It's a humble reminder that we are poor judges of impact. We simply entrust our lives and words to God and let Him use them as He pleases, often in secret.

4. THE DISCIPLINE OF SINGING

Many times in Scripture, particularly the Psalms, we're encouraged to sing. But sometimes I fear I've lost my voice. Have you felt that way?

In *Hinds' Feet on High Places* by Hannah Hurnard, Much-Afraid, a scarred and scared woman, tries to venture to the high places. In this point in her journey mountainward, she travels in the mist, nothing around her but her companions Sorrow and Suffering. And everywhere she walks, she hears the voices of her enemies trying to discourage and destroy her. Finally, after the voices threaten to stop her, she decides to sing. Hurnard wrote, "There was perfect silence as she sang. The loud, sneering voices of her enemies had died away altogether. 'It is a good idea,' said Much-Afraid to herself jubilantly. 'I wish I had thought of it before. It [singing] is a much better way to avoid hearing what they are saying than putting cotton in my ears, and I believe, yes, I really do believe, there is a little rift in the mist ahead. How lovely, I shall sing the verse again.' And she did so."[3]

When we make a choice to sing even though we don't feel like it, He creates something supernatural in our lives.

This touched me. It reminded me that God encourages us to sing. Particularly when the voices inside and around yell terrible things. We discipline ourselves from stifling the song ourselves, being brave enough to sing to Jesus. We have much to sing about, much for which to thank God: "I will shout for joy and sing your praises, for you have ransomed me" (Ps. 71:23 NLT).

No matter what swirls around your life, the truth is God has ransomed you. He is bigger than the naysayers. When we make a choice to sing even though we don't feel like it, He creates something supernatural in our lives. Sometimes when I'm particularly down or needy or small, I ignite my worship playlist and have at it. And as I do, reflecting not on my situation, but on God's adequacy to love me through it, the day changes. All because of song.

5. THE DISCIPLINE OF GRATITUDE

My friend Ann Voskamp wrote the startling book *One Thousand Gifts* that perfectly woos us all toward gratitude. Though in a similar vein as singing, gratitude is not a discipline that comes easily to me. I tend toward pessimism (which I'd rather call realism). Even today as I lamented my paycheck, I stopped myself and chose to remember that

God has enabled my husband to make a suitable salary. When I did that, my funk disappeared. We're like the Israelites, murmuring in their tents:

> They despised the pleasant land,
>   having no faith in his promise.
> They murmured in their tents,
>   and did not obey the voice of the LORD. (Ps. 106:24–25)

All that murmuring must've grieved God, yet I see my own murmuring ways. I long to shout this verse loud enough so I believe it, really believe it: "I believe that I shall look upon the goodness of the LORD in the land of the living!" (Ps. 27:13). Today, right now, we have a choice to exercise this discipline of gratitude. Either we can focus wholly on our issues and problems, or we can take on a posture of gratitude toward our holy God.

Gratitude recognizes that everything we have—our talents, our relationships, our things—comes from God (James 1:17). Even our growth emanates from Him: "Neither he who plants nor he who waters is anything, but only God who gives the growth" (1 Cor. 3:7). Living, breathing, walking, seeing, touching, tasting, loving—all a gift: "What gives you the right to make such a judgment? What do you have that God hasn't given you? And if everything you have is from God, why boast as though it were not a gift?" (1 Cor. 4:7 NLT).

God has given so many gifts, but we pass them by like ungrateful children on Christmas. The discipline of gratitude chooses to stop, to notice, to open the gift and thank the Giver.

6. THE DISCIPLINE OF SILENCE

Sometimes I'm loud when it comes to my reputation. I've lived for micromanaging my reputation, forgetting to let God be in control. I'm learning to let go of what people think of me. To let negative opinions (whether they are accurate or not) roll away. Still, it's not easy. I'd rather run around like a crazy woman letting everyone know that I'm not what someone thinks I am, that my sum total is better, more laudable. But then I only look oddly guilty. And it expends energy I should be expending for Jesus and His kingdom.

In this pace of worry, I'm learning to exercise the discipline of silence. I remember Jesus saying not. one. word. before His accusers, when He certainly had a right to. His silence, no doubt, unnerved them. But He had such a heart so well connected to the Father that He knew He lived for the audience of One, not the audience of the crowd. Oh, to live like that! A. B. Simpson summarizes this discipline:

> There is a place of stillness that allows God the opportunity to work for us and give us peace. It is a stillness that ceases our scheming self-vindication, and the search for a temporary means to an end through our own wisdom and judgment. Instead, it lets God provide an answer, through His unfailing and faithful love, to the cruel blow we have suffered. Oh how often we thwart God's intervention on our behalf by taking up our own cause or by striking a blow in our own defense! May God grant each of us this silent power and submissive spirit.[4]

Yes, may He grant us all the discipline of silence—that same silence He personified. May Peter's declaration about Jesus' silence be true in our lives as well: "When they hurled their insults at him, he did not retaliate; when he suffered, he made no threats. Instead, he entrusted himself to him who judges justly" (1 Peter 2:23 NIV).

7. THE DISCIPLINE OF FORGIVENESS

If you want to stifle your growth—stop yourself dead on the path—coddle a critical, unforgiving heart. The cancer of unforgiveness, if not rooted out, routs your growth and renders you bitter. Yes, it's true that you've been hurt, maybe wrongly accused. You've experienced injustice. People who were supposed to love and protect you did neither. Others might have deliberately harmed you. You may have enemies. Still others did not live up to your expectations. They have neglected you or not cared enough.

Whatever the offense, we've all experienced deep wounds at the hands of people, often those we love fiercely.

Still, forgiveness is a discipline. It comes through our vehicle of choice. God commands it, which should pause us right now in order to evaluate why we're unwilling to forgive. From the cross, Jesus uttered those

The cancer of unforgiveness, if not rooted out, routs your growth and renders you bitter.

forgiving words to the ones who crucified Him. And He asks us to do the same. To be a follower of Jesus, we must do what He did. We are more like Him when we forgive.

Forgiving is not the same as forgetting. We do remember the offense. We call it evil. We rightly say that what happened was egregious. And then, with God's help, we let it go. We place the person who hurt us in God's hands, not our own. Because if we hold on to that person and the hurt he or she forced upon us, our grip will close, and we'll live tight-fisted, hard-hearted lives. Learning the discipline of forgiveness helps us to reorient our pasts. In the light of letting go of our red vengeance, we begin to see the past as a gift, a place where Jesus walked alongside us, even if we weren't aware of His footfalls then. If we choose not to forgive, we chain ourselves to the moment of the pain, and we seldom grow beyond it.

8. The Discipline of Creativity

We serve a creative God who brings variety and change and beauty to us every day. He is creativity personified. Yet we forsake newness and innovation in the way we approach Him. We rely on staid quiet times, rote prayers, worship services tainted by sameness. It's my heart right now to see you become free in the way you interact with Jesus. Don't settle for uniformity. Paint your joy. Sing your prayer. Run under a wide blue sky, counting your blessings. Explore your world alongside Him. Chronicle the beauty of the earth through the lens of your camera. Serve the downtrodden, believing you'll see Jesus as you do.

What I find inspiring: our wildly creative God made each of us different, so of course we connect with Him in varied ways. Take some time this week to pray about what makes your heart sing. Chances are the way you best connect to God jumped out at you as you read the sentences above. If you're feeling spiritually dry and disconnected, take some time to do the very thing that invigorates you. Take a hike. Spend time alone. Study your Bible. Sing to Jesus. Serve others. Create something. Find some community. Be creative in the way you approach God. Live in joyful anticipation of His holy intersections.

Make a choice today to be the creative person He made you to be. Let go of your "what you're supposed to do to grow" list, and permit God to make the list. This life in Christ is a daring adventure, full of beauty and surprise. Why not let the God of the universe lead even your time with Him?

9. THE DISCIPLINE OF REST

Currently I teeter on the edge of burnout. I'm poured out. Thirsty. Straining for words. Sometimes losing my mind. In the past seven years, I've written twenty-one books—three full-length books a year. This doesn't include all my blog posts or articles. A rough estimate where the average book length is 70,000 words, blog posts 400 words, and articles 1,000 words, I've written more than 3,082,000 words the past seven years.

How about you? Are you so burned out you can't think about engaging with a needy friend? Does doing something outside your comfort zone scare you precisely because it will take more energy than you have? Do you think of ways you can get so sick you'll have to be hospitalized, just so you can sit in a bed, have no expectations thrust on you, and watch TV for hours on end? I've been there. I am there.

Real growth doesn't happen in a rush. It can't flourish in burnout. It takes introspection, time, and a balanced, healthy life. Michael Yaconelli kicked my behind when he wrote, "Spiritual growth is not running faster, as in more meetings, more Bible studies, and more prayer meetings. Spiritual growth happens when we slow our activity down. If we want to meet Jesus, we can't do it on the run. If we want to stay on the road of faith, we have to hit the brakes, pull over to a rest area, and stop. Christianity is not about inviting Jesus to speed through life with us; it's about noticing Jesus at the rest stop."[5]

How can we grow if we never slow down to spend time with our Savior? How can we thrive if our lives are full of frenetic energy? We've become like Israel when the Lord through Isaiah warned,

> *Only in returning to me*
> *and resting in me will you be saved.*
> *In quietness and confidence is your strength.*
> *But you would have none of it.*
> *You said, "No, we will get our help from Egypt.*
> *They will give us swift horses for riding into battle."*
> *But the only swiftness you are going to see*
> *is the swiftness of your enemies chasing you!* (Isa. 30:15–16 NLT)

Only in returning to Jesus and learning how to rest in Him will we grow, receiving as a side benefit confidence and strength. We often try to "get our help from Egypt." Egypt was Israel's place of exile and slavery, yet the Israelites longed for it much like we long for enslavement to an overstressed life. We don't run to God, collapsing on His grace. We run to things that will quicken us, make us more productive.

Growth happens in the soil of our lives where darkness and quiet and stillness reign. On our own, we try to grow quickly, pushing ourselves from the soil to the light of busy day, thinking we're smart for doing so. Instead, in the light of the sun, we wither, then wonder why. God is not fast. He does not encourage us to kick life into high gear. Jesus walked everywhere; He didn't run. He lived a settled, unhurried life. He took long stretches of time away from crowds, communing with His Father. In that, He learned the Father's directives for the days and weeks to come. He became wholly interruptible, alive in each moment, attentive to the whispers of God wherever He ventured. If we want to live a grow-like-crazy life like His, we must slow down like crazy.

> *Growth happens in the soil of our lives where darkness and quiet and stillness reign.*

In our instant-conversion-to-ministry culture, we forget the years it took before Jesus stepped onto the stage of humanity—thirty to be exact. And Paul, after his conversion, didn't rush into working for Jesus. Instead he exiled himself, learning about the Way, living outcasted. He didn't rush into service until God revealed it was time, a period of over seventeen years between his Damascus road light show to the time he entered public ministry (Gal. 1–2). Yet somehow we think that the moment we experience something surprising or redemptive, we must instantly share it with everyone. Could it be that God calls us first to ponder and think through the implications of His actions on our behalf?

One way to determine God's timing is to instigate the holy practice of Sabbath living. The best book I've read on this topic is *The Rest of God* by Mark Buchanan. This perspective on Sabbath has revolutionized the way I view ministry and work and rest. Unfortunately, as I mentioned at the beginning of this section, I fall back on busyness and production. Why? Because the culture we breathe and work in rushes against rest. It equates our worth with production and wealth and fame. The more we work toward those goals, the more society assigns us worth.

So I'm splashing Buchanan's words on my tired face again. He woos us toward Sabbath, taking a day off a week for holy rejuvenation: "Sabbath is time sanctified, time betrothed, time we perceive and receive and approach differently from all other time. Sabbath time is unlike every and any other time on the clock and the calendar. We are more intimate with it. We are more thankful for it. We are more protective of it and generous with it. We become more ourselves in the presence of Sabbath: more vulnerable, less afraid. More ready to confess, to be silent, to be small, to be valiant."[6]

I don't feel valiant today, but the longing resides in me—a hope that my life will count for eternity, that my relationships will reflect my ability to be interrupted. I want to be more like Jesus, purposeful with my time and intentional with my rest. I need to remember the wisdom of Proverbs and deliberately take time alone to be watered by Jesus: "Whoever brings blessing will be enriched, and one who waters will himself be watered" (Prov. 11:25).

What about you? What story do you tell? Is your life a thriller with no pauses, constant turmoil, and little margin on the page? Do you tell the story of burnout by the way you live? Does the thought of resting for a week, completely unplugged, both terrify and entice you? It may be that God has called you to Himself to rest, refuel, and rejuvenate. He may be beckoning you to a retreat where you can reassess your life and find yourself again.

Knowing when you're spent is no sign of weakness; it's pure grace and strength. Because we cannot live this Christian life in our own strength or we'll be constantly prone to fail. As I quoted earlier, Jesus said, "Yes, I am the vine; you are the branches. Those who remain in me, and I in them, will produce much fruit. For apart from me you can do nothing" (John 15:5 NLT). Nothing. Nothing. Nothing. Not one thing.

10. The Discipline of Spiritual Warfare

This world is not what it seems. We have a very real enemy who wants to destroy us and lie to us. Satan was "a murderer from the beginning, and does not stand in the truth because there is no truth in him. Whenever he speaks a lie, he speaks from his own nature, for he is a liar and the father of lies" (John 8:44 NASB). Jesus highlighted the destructiveness of Satan when He said, "The thief's purpose is to steal and kill and destroy. My purpose is to give them a rich and satisfying life" (John 10:10 NLT). Remember the latter half of that verse, that, yes, Satan wants to steal from us, but Jesus wants to give us abundance.

The longer we walk with Jesus, the subtler Satan becomes in his attempt to trip us up.

Paul experienced Satan's opposition as well: "We wanted very much to come to you, and I, Paul, tried again and again, but Satan prevented us" (1 Thess. 2:18 NLT). So if Jesus warned us about Satan's nature and Paul experienced Satan's thwarting, we must take the threat seriously.

The longer we walk with Jesus, the subtler Satan becomes in his attempt to trip us up. In the beginning, he may resort to grandiose displays of himself, trying to freak us out. But as we begin to see him in the obvious ways, he becomes cleverer, more alert to our weaknesses. In our mature years of knowing Jesus, the Enemy becomes a no-see-um gnat, barely detectable, but still with a bite.

The most insidious of his ploys involves using others to deflate and destroy us, people we think of as believers. Paul warned, "These people are false apostles. They are deceitful workers who disguise themselves as apostles of Christ. But I am not surprised! Even Satan disguises himself as an angel of light. So it is no wonder that his servants also disguise themselves as servants of righteousness. In the end they will get the punishment their wicked deeds deserve" (2 Cor. 11:13–15 NLT). Some of the most painful, discouraging times in my walk with Jesus have come when those who have said they were Christians acted in deceit and cunning. When other Christians hurt us, we have a choice: let their antics derail us, or choose to forgive and move on. The latter is pure spiritual warfare.

The supremacy of God trumps Satan every time. He is bigger, more powerful, all-knowing—the sovereign King of the universe. Resting in His capability instead of our stealth will help us rely on the One capable of winning spiritual battles. In order to grow, we must settle this issue of God's greatness. He has the power to do great things, secure victories, and save many:

> Sing a new song to the LORD,
>   for he has done wonderful deeds.
> His right hand has won a mighty victory;
>   his holy arm has shown his saving power! (Ps. 98:1 NLT)

He lives in the heavens, exalted and all-powerful, yet He chooses to commune with us, particularly if we're humble:

> The high and lofty one who lives in eternity,
>   the Holy One, says this:
> "I live in the high and holy place
>   with those whose spirits are contrite and humble.
> I restore the crushed spirit of the humble
>   and revive the courage of those with repentant hearts."
> (Isa. 57:15 NLT)

Though Satan despises our weakness, lies to us, and wants to destroy us, God promises to be with us, reviving our courage. In the book of Romans, Paul summed up God's ability to help us: "What then shall we say to these things? If God is for us, who can be against us? He who did not spare his own Son but gave him up for us all, how will he not also with him graciously give us all things? Who shall bring any charge against God's elect? It is God who justifies. Who is to condemn? Christ Jesus is the one who died—more than that, who was raised—who is at the right hand of God, who indeed is interceding for us" (8:31–34).

With the all-knowing, all-powerful, all-seeing God battling on our behalf, we need not fear our enemy. We simply become aware of the Enemy, then trust in God's might.

• • •

There is beauty in discipline; there is a freedom. As I've studied writing and the kernel of genius, I've learned a secret: great work flows from hours of hard work. Malcolm Gladwell in his book *Outliers* says that brilliance comes from a not-so-magic number: ten thousand hours. What you're reading today are words strung together based on twenty years of practice and discipline. Why do we expect outstanding results from little effort? Why do we expect spiritual growth without the daily-ness of choosing to follow Jesus no matter what He asks? Our growth comes in these small obediences over the long haul of our sanctification journey.

When we watch the life of Jesus, we see His discipline, of pulling away from crowds, of investing in the least of these as the Father led. At twelve years old, He stood in the temple, discoursing with the rabbis, studying Scripture. His life became pure worship, sacrificial servant-hood. If Jesus disciplined Himself like this, we must step into His footsteps. That's what being a follower of Jesus means—to walk wherever He leads, even if that journey means we lay aside our agendas, get our hands dirty, or take time away from this crazy life.

Your growth depends on choices made today, choices married to the power of the Holy Spirit within you. They determine whether you will grow or stagnate. My prayer for you as you live this disciplined, joyful life is Paul's prayer:

When I think of all this, I fall to my knees and pray to the Father, the Creator of everything in heaven and on earth. I pray that from his glorious, unlimited resources he will empower you with inner strength through his Spirit. Then Christ will make his home in your hearts as you trust in him. Your roots will grow down into God's love and keep you strong. And may you have the power to understand, as all God's people should, how wide, how long, how high, and how deep his love is. May you experience the love of Christ, though it is too great to understand fully. Then you will be made complete with all the fullness of life and power that comes from God. Now all glory to God, who is able, through his mighty power at work within us, to accomplish infinitely more than we might ask or think. Glory to him in the church and in Christ Jesus through all generations forever and ever! Amen. (Eph. 3:14–21 NLT)

Yes, amen.

QUESTIONS FOR REFLECTION AND DISCUSSION

- What disciplines in this chapter do you struggle to keep? Which come easily to you?

- How often do you think about spiritual warfare? What's been your experience with the dark forces of this world in the past three months?

- Who do you need to forgive?

- In what areas of your life do you need to rest?

- When have you relegated creativity to the back burner of your life? When have you welcomed it?

The Everything Life

Welcome to the living Stone, the source of life.

—1 PETER 2:4 MSG

HOW CAN WE, PEOPLE WEIGHED DOWN BY INSECURITY AND sin and stress, live like Jesus? How can we possibly rise above our past, our failure, or our preconceived notions of what we should be (but aren't)? If it weren't for Jesus Himself, we couldn't. We can't. We won't be able to.

Jesus is the pathway to the Everything life. He walked this earth in a winsome, beautiful, evocative way. He revealed the Father's redemptive heart to this sin-blackened world. He modeled being a servant and giving up one's will. In His perfection and love, He willingly gave His life so we could be set free from the penalty of sin. Jesus bled for us. He conquered the enemy of death. He crushed Satan and his evil intentions. He ushered in the era of the Holy Spirit. And He welcomes us all to live like Him through the Spirit's power.

- Which is why we can't and He can.
- Which is why an Everything life has more to do with surrender than personal triumph.

This world doesn't covet our intelligence. It doesn't need our wit or wherewithal. It has no use for our coy phraseologies. It needs Jesus—full of outrageous grace, unconditional love, and hope-filled pardon. And it needs Him this moment.

The Great Right Now beckons us. The irresistible future woos. We cannot change the past, but we can live joyfully in the present and look expectantly to the future. All because of Jesus.

The past is for lessons, for discerning Jesus' hand and how He grew us. It's not the place to dwell or stay stuck. As I penned this book, for the first time in five years post-France, I started having memories of our time there. And not all of them were painful. God gave me these holy glimpses to remind me that healing does come, in time. All that growth that incubated in French soil had a purpose somehow. All that bewilderment, that bereavement, meant something. As I remember walking my kids to school under a pristine sky, wide tree branches brushing against a stone chapel, I remember the intimacy Jesus and I cultivated there. He had to be my everything when I felt like nothing. He had to be my sustenance when my soul starved and everything crumbled around me. He had to hold my hand when I couldn't see it in front of me through all that darkness.

Here is the secret of growing right now—holding Jesus' hand as we walk the paths He stretches before us.

Here is the secret of growing right now—holding Jesus' hand as we walk the paths He stretches before us. How we choose to live in each moment is actually the manner we live our lives. Think about that a minute or two or sixty.

Maybe you're a bit like me. I'm two Marys. Everything Mary wishes to live a radical life, a life of great dependence on Jesus Christ, a life of deep connection with others, a life of unrestrained worship—where I truly give Jesus everything. Then there's Reality Mary, the Mary of the daily life. She's not all that. She's needy, ordinary, beset, and flimsy. The fundamental place we grow is in the moment-by-moment decisions we make for or against Jesus in our lives. In this moment you're reading these words stark on a page, you have the choice to grow, and He has the ability to meet that choice with the power and strength and cheerleading and unfettered love to make it happen. He has the wherewithal to grow you, not in a measurable A to B trajectory, but in a multiplying, inside-out way—the kind of growth that's difficult to measure.

This life of loving Jesus is meant to be joyful, surprising—an incredible journey. He has so much prepared for you. Don't let fear or the need to control every single thing in your life prevent you from abandoning everything to Him. Because Jesus is worth it. He is everything. He rescued you from sin's grip on your affections, from having to prove your worth, from your past. He healed you, set your feet on rock, and gave you reason to rejoice. He gave you a better example beyond the bitter hatred, fighting, and strife in this world.

Don't let fear or the need to control every single thing in your life prevent you from abandoning everything to Him.

And today He lives. The Great I Am. The Great Right Now. The One worthy of all adoration, affection, and allegiance. He lives.

As you close the covers on our time together, go with this Scripture that touts the beauty of Jesus. Read these words as if they're fresh, new, bold. Let them wash over you, inspiring you to live differently:

As you come to him, a living stone rejected by men but in the sight of God chosen and precious, you yourselves like living stones are being built up as a spiritual house, to be a holy priesthood, to offer spiritual sacrifices acceptable to God through Jesus Christ. For it stands in Scripture:

"Behold, I am laying in Zion a stone,
   a cornerstone chosen and precious,
   and whoever believes in him will not be put to shame."

So the honor is for you who believe, but for those who do not believe,

"The stone that the builders rejected
   has become the cornerstone,"

and

"A stone of stumbling,
   and a rock of offense."

They stumble because they disobey the word, as they were destined to do.

But you are a chosen race, a royal priesthood, a holy nation, a people for his own possession, that you may proclaim the excellencies of him who called you out of darkness into his marvelous light. Once you were not a people, but now you are God's people; once you had not received mercy, but now you have received mercy. (1 Peter 2:4–10)

In light of that great truth, as dearly loved and accepted people, may we dare to believe that Jesus is big enough to grow us today. That our lives would become wide enough to trust Him for big things, new ventures, a brand-new future, for everything. May we spend our moments loving Him and loving others. My prayer for you is that Jesus will become your everything.

Not for your fame, but for His sake and renown.

Amen.

❧ Acknowledgments

PATRICK, IT'S YOUR MIND AND YOUR GREAT TEACHING that inspired this book. You demonstrate an Everything life in such infectious ways. Thank you.

Hugs to my children, Sophie, Aidan, and Julia, who demonstrate Jesus and His love and grace to me every day. I love you all. I'm inspired by each one of you.

Thank you, Leslie Wilson and D'Ann Mateer, who gave expert editorial advice on this manuscript.

Thank you to the amazing staff at Thomas Nelson. Bryan Norman, I tear up every time I think about our first phone conversation. It means more than I can articulate that you believe in me and cheer me on.

Esther Fedorkevich, you've been exactly what I needed when I felt like giving up this writing gig thing. Every time I faltered, your voice on the other end of the phone told me to keep going, keep trying, keep turning over those rocks. So I did. And here we are. And I'm not a Walmart greeter.

My prayer team is a gift to me in so many ways. Thanks for the advice, prayers, and unsolicited encouragement as I wrote this book. I love you all! Twilla Fontenot, Ashley Weis, Kevin and Renee Bailey, Carla Smith, Caroline Coleman, Cheramy Mayfield, Colleen Eslinger, Jeanne Damoff, Darren and Holly Sapp, D'Ann Mateer, Dorian Coover-Cox, Erin Teske, Katy Gedney, Kimberly Baker, Ginger Vassar, Helen Graves, Holly Schmidt, Jan Winebrenner, Jen Powell, Kathy ONeall, Katy Raymond, Denise Willhite, Anita Curtis, Diane Klapper, Lesley Hamilton, Leslie Wilson, Lilli Brenchley, Liz Wolf, Marcia Robbins, Marcus Goodyear, Grace Bower, Marybeth Whalen, Pam LeTourneau, Paula Moldenhauer, Rae McIlrath, Phyllis Yount, Becky Ochs, Sandi Glahn, Sarah Walker, Shawna Marie Bryant, Tim Riter, Tina Howard, Tracy Walker, Heidi Van Dyken, Paul Napari, Renee Mills, Stacey Tomisser, John Davis, Carla Williams, Nicole Baart, Tosca Lee, Marilyn Scholtz, TJ Wilson, Jim Rubart, Patrick DeMuth, Jody Capehart, Susan Meissner, Ariel Lawhon, Mary Vestal, Amy Sorrells, Lisa Shea, Dena Dyer, Kathryn Thomas, Carol Avery, Cyndi Kraweitz, Don Pape, Esther Fedorkevich, Susie Larson, Christy Tennant, Jodi Vinson, and Ericka Smiley.

To the DeMuth advisory board, thank you for your wisdom, listening ear, and sage advice: Randy Ingermanson, Jody Capeheart, Holly Schmidt, Cathleen Lewis, Kimberly Baker, Stacey Tomisser, Denise Martin, Patrick DeMuth, Pam LeTourneau, Heidi Van Dyken, Alice Crider, Leslie Wilson, and D'Ann Mateer.

Jesus, You are everything. And everything is You.

ᓚ Notes

Preface: *The Everything Journey*
 1. Michael Yaconelli, *Messy Spirituality: God's Annoying Love for Imperfect People* (Grand Rapids, MI: Zondervan, 2002), 97.
 2. Barna Group, "Research on How God Transforms Lives Reveals a 10-Stop Journey," March 17, 2011, http://www.barna.org/ transformation-articles/480-research-on-how-god-transforms-lives-reveals-a-10-stop-journey.

Chapter 1: *Cultivate the Discipline of Astonishment*
 1. David Platt, *Radical: Taking Your Faith Back from the American Dream* (Colorado Springs: Multnomah, 2011), 46–47.
 2. T. Austin Sparks, *The School of Christ*, http://www.austin-sparks.net/ english/books/001033.html.
 3. For a longer exploration of this story, see *Beautiful Battle* (Eugene, OR: Harvest House, 2012).

Chapter 2: *Live the Six-Letter Word That Changes Everything*
 1. Kyle Idleman, "Not a Fan of Jesus," *Neue*, August/September 2011, 47.
 2. I was first introduced to this concept at a church planting seminar headed up by Bob Roberts Junior.
 3. Ibid.

Chapter 3: Discern the Vow Factor

1. Mary DeMuth, *Building the Christian Family You Never Had* (Colorado Springs: WaterBrook Press, 2006), 45.

Chapter 4: Let Go of the Giants

1. Madame Guyon, http://christian-quotes.ochristian.com/Madame-Guyon-Quotes/page-2.shtml.

2. Oswald Chambers, *My Utmost for His Highest* (Westwood, NJ: Barbour and Company, 1935), January 11.

3. Ibid., June 13.

4. Dietrich Bonhoeffer, *The Cost of Discipleship* (New York: Macmillan, 1937), 36.

Chapter 5: Set Aside Worry

1. David McCasland, *Oswald Chambers: Abandoned to God* (Grand Rapids, MI: Discover House Books, 1993), 194–95.

Chapter 6: Practice Resilience

1. "Resilience," http://www.merriam-webster.com/dictionary/resilience.

2. Oswald Chambers, *My Utmost for His Highest* (Westwood, NJ: Barbour and Company, 1935), October 21.

Chapter 7: Be an Am

1. Bob George, *Classic Christianity: Life's Too Short to Miss the Real Thing* (Eugene, OR: Harvest House, 1989), 58.

2. C. H. Spurgeon, "Surely He Shall Deliver Thee from the Snare of the Fowler," http://www.sermonindex.net/modules/articles/index.php?view=article&aid=5168.

Chapter 8: Forsake the Seven-Letter Word That Demolishes Everything

1. Bob George, *Classic Christianity: Life's Too Short to Miss the Real Thing* (Eugene, OR: Harvest House, 1989), 109.

Chapter 10: Choose to Heal

1. E-mail to the author, August 22, 2011.

2. L. B. Cowman, *Streams in the Desert* (Grand Rapids, MI: Zondervan, 1997), January 20.

3. Sue Monk Kidd, *The Secret Life of Bees* (New York: Penguin Group, 2002), 3.

Chapter 11: Lean into Brokenness

1. Madame Guyon, http://christian-quotes.ochristian.com/Madame-Guyon-Quotes/.
2. Oswald Chambers, *My Utmost for His Highest* (Westwood, NJ: Barbour and Company, 1935), December 2.

Chapter 12: Be Kind to Yourself

1. Timothy Ferriss, *The 4-Hour Workweek* (New York: Crown Publishers, 2010), 256.
2. "Examen," http://ignatianspirituality.com/ignatian-prayer/the-examen/.
3. Mike Mason, *Practicing the Presence of People* (Colorado Springs: WaterBrook Press, 1999), 73.

Chapter 13: Relinquish Money

1. Randy Alcorn, *The Treasure Principle* (Sister, OR: Multnomah, 2001), 20.
2. Ibid., 93.

Chapter 14: Reconcile the Paradox of Failure

1. As quoted in Leonard Roy Frank, *Quotationary* (New York: Random House, 2001), 265, from "Life in a Love," l. 13.
2. L. B. Cowman, *Streams in the Desert* (Grand Rapids, MI: Zondervan, 1997), June 11.

Chapter 15: Grow Better Together

1. As quoted in L. B. Cowman, *Streams in the Desert* (Grand Rapids, MI: Zondervan, 1997), July 29.

Chapter 16: Follow the Leader

1. George Barna, *Maximum Faith* (Glendora, CA: WHC Publishing, 2011), 36.
2. Barna Group, "Research on How God Transforms Lives Reveals a 10-Stop Journey," March 17, 2011, http://www.barna.org/transformation-articles/480-research-on-how-god-transforms-lives-reveals-a-10-stop-journey.
3. A. W. Tozer, *The Knowledge of the Holy* (San Francisco, CA: HarperOne, 1978), 1.
4. David Platt, *Radical: Taking Your Faith Back from the American Dream* (Colorado Springs: Multnomah, 2011), 73.

5. David McCasland, *Oswald Chambers: Abandoned to God* (Grand Rapids, MI: Discover House Books, 1993), 109.
6. Ibid., 59.

Chapter 17: Become Irresistible
1. Mother Teresa, http://thinkexist.com/quotation/the_most_terrible_poverty_is_loneliness_and_the/216333.html.
2. Dietrich Bonhoeffer, *Life Together: The Classic Exploration of Christian Community* (San Francisco, CA: HarperOne, 1978), 99.

Chapter 18: Walk Out Surprising Disciplines
1. As quoted in L. B. Cowman, *Streams in the Desert* (Grand Rapids, MI: Zondervan, 1997), August 15.
2. For a better explanation of eternal perspective, read any of Randy Alcorn's books.
3. Hannah Hurnard, *Hinds' Feet on High Places* (Grand Rapids, MI: Tyndale House, 1975), 162.
4. As quoted in Cowman, *Streams in the Desert*, April 5.
5. Michael Yaconelli, *Messy Spirituality: God's Annoying Love for Imperfect People* (Grand Rapids, MI: Zondervan, 2002), 88.
6. Mark Buchanan, *The Rest of God: Restoring Your Soul by Restoring Sabbath* (Nashville: Thomas Nelson, 2007), 35.

MARY DEMUTH IS AN AUTHOR AND SPEAKER WHO LOVES to help people live uncaged, freedom-infused lives. She's the author of fourteen books, including six novels and her critically acclaimed memoir, *Thin Places*. After church planting in Southern France, Mary, her husband, and their three teenagers now live in a suburb of Dallas. Find out more at:

marydemuth.com
EverythingTheBook.com
#EverythingBook

Everything
Join the Community

If you've experienced life change or a shift in your perspective after reading *Everything*, I'd love to hear your story. Here are some avenues you can share your "everything" discoveries with everyone.

—Mary

 Twitter: @MaryDeMuth   **hashtag:** #EverythingBook

 Facebook: Facebook.com/authormarydemuth

 Pinterest: http://pinterest.com/mary_demuth/everything-book/

Web: EverythingTheBook.com

E-mail: mary@marydemuth.com

 Tweets about the book:

@karen_ehman: "Just finished @MaryDeMuth 's new book #EverythingBook. Can't wait to write an endorsement. It rocketh :-)"

@CharlesSpecht: "If we have a low view of God, we will not go to Him for help or wisdom." @MaryDeMuth #Everythingbook/

 Shared on Facebook:

Katherine Harms: "Just finished Mary DeMuth's *Everything*. This book is a must-read for everyone serious about growing in relationship with Christ. I'm going to recommend it for my study group after the current series."